ROGER POOLE

TOWARDS
DEEP
SUBJECTIVITY

Harper & Row, Publishers
New York, Evanston, San Francisco, London

Acknowledgments are due to the following for permission to reproduce photographs: *Le Figaro* (page VIII-1) and Time-Life, Inc. (pages 8-9).

LIBRARY OF CONGRESS CATALOGUE CARD NUMBER: 72-82896

STANDARD BOOK NUMBER: 06-131676-8 (PAPERBACK)

STANDARD BOOK NUMBER: 06-136077-5 (HARDCOVER)

CONTENTS

1   Ethical Space   3
2   Subjectivity as Expression in the World   12
3   'Objectivity'   44
4   Subjective Objections to 'Objectivity'   78
5   The Perspectival World and Subjective
        Method   113
6   Philosophical Space   140

Its beginning course is necessarily one of experiencing and thinking in naïve self-evidence. It possesses no formed logic and methodology in advance and can achieve its method and even the genuine sense of its accomplishments only through ever-renewed self-reflections. Its fate (understood subsequently, to be sure, as an essentially necessary one) is to become involved again and again in paradoxes, which, arising out of uninvestigated and even unnoticed horizons, remain functional and announce themselves as incomprehensibilities.

Husserl, *The Crisis of European Sciences and Transcendental Phenomenology*

1

ETHICAL
SPACE

Three Russian soldiers and four Czech citizens are sitting on park benches in Prague. The time is late summer 1968.

The three Russians sit in a row, staring before them. One of them has leant his weapon casually against his knee. Further along the bench, two Czech citizens are bent forward, staring at the ground.

At right angles to the Russians, a young man and a girl are sitting. Both of them are looking at the Russians. Both are immobile, reflective. The young man stares directly at the Russians, who all three take care to avoid his glance. The girl looks at the Russians only obliquely, her eyes covering them in swift forays. The Russians stare ahead of them, creating a kind of neutral space where their looks cannot be intercepted.

They seem less the aggressors, the Russians, than unwilling guests at an execution. No doubt they can see what the young Czechs would like to say, do say indeed in their posture and attitude.

The Russians indeed appear to have considerable sympathy for them. The Russian with the gun would not like to have to use it. He hopes that his fellow Communists in

Prague will not show so much bad taste as to force him to use it. He wishes to be accepted as a human being before he is classed as a Russian soldier and liberator.

The inability of the Russians to enter into conversation with the Czechs is not only linguistic: it is part and parcel of the historical situation. They are seen as Russians and they are submitted to Czech scrutiny.

The square, the park, the benches, all are Czech.

The Russians were not invited here, they forced their way into that park and into all other parks and streets in the city. They shot their way in, they tanked their way in. Now they are in.

And they are faced with a problem: the space of Prague remains Czech. Resolutely, determinedly, Czech. The space of the park benches is claimed by the young Czech citizens as *theirs*. This space is Czech space.

The Russians do not seriously try to deny this, not these Russians at any rate. For the truth of the situation is most forcibly carried in the posture and bodily expressiveness of the two young people opposite them.

Those postures convey a certain message much more powerfully than any words could.

Just as the bodily pose of the Russian with the rifle allowed of a certain interpretation, so the pose of the young man is equally expressive of a thought-process.

'By what right do you sit there, Ivan, with your gun against your knee? By what curious logic do you appeal not to be regarded as an invader, when by your very presence you are denying us our rights to this space?'

The human body can, in its silent presence, convey a complete moral attitude, can implicitly deny the rightness of what is going on.

It is for this reason that the Russians keep their look resolutely in front of them, where the space is freed of intercepting moral judgements.

The space in question is divided up ethically simply through the directions of the looks of the people there.

The three Russians lay claim to one third of the space each, so to speak. They do not claim the whole of it. They merely claim the right to sit in it for a moment.

But that division of the space of the park is challenged by the young Czechs. The *whole* space is claimed for Czech citizens.

None of it is to be occupied on this temporary basis, where the moral status of the space has been annulled by force. The space is already tending back towards Czech ownership.

Only by avoiding the glances of the young Czechs can the Russians avoid acceding to this queer spatial property.

Only by avoiding their glance can the suspension of Czech space be maintained. For that suspension is dependent upon the immobility of the young Czech man and girl. The suspension is a result of the Czech tact, which accords to the Russians some human comprehension even while it judges their presence here as quite inadmissible.

The Russians occupy the space against the will of the owners of the space, but are yet immobilized in it. It is a foreign, hostile medium.

The Czechs are physically prisoners in their own space, but not morally so. The inverse is true of the Russians. The space which is occupied is still not owned.

The Czechs are prisoners in objective space but free in subjective space. Again the Russians occupy the inverse position.

The ethical properties of this space are easy to decipher: both Czechs and Russians in their physical immobility testify to their ethical impotence to act impersonally in the space set out before them.

Any action whatsoever undertaken in that divided space between the three Russians and the two Czechs would be subject to comment from the Czechs present in the park. We can see four, no doubt there are more. There is no action that the Russians could undertake which would not be subject to drastic interpretation. Even their sitting down is resented.

The space spread out before the protagonists of the drama is ethical space itself.

Meaning and interpretation belong together inseparably. Anything which visibly has a meaning is in that same instant invested with an interpretation by each and every onlooker.

There can be no flaccid action, no action which is not immediately imbued with an ethical ballast, filled in from our point of view in the world of perspectives.

The meaning attributed to what goes on in the significant space before our eyes will vary according to our moral presuppositions, the partial vision we receive, the position we occupy in the perspectival world.

Interpretation will always be instantaneous. We are never conscious of a split second of time intervening between what we see and the moral account we give of it.

Acts in space are embodied intentions.

The first elements of a grammar and rhetoric of the visual world need to be strung together, a grammar and rhetoric of the ethically embodied act.

To take account of what an act is significant of is not enough : we need to advance to the point of understanding what it signifies and what it is intended to signify.

An ethical grammar of the visual would begin by connecting the signifier of the acts in space with the signified which is the intention of the actor. Obviously this is not and can never be achieved by quantitative analysis.

In the park in Prague, two sorts of space intersect. There are two sorts of space because there are two sorts of intentions plainly visible in the photograph. The intentions structure the space in two different ways.

When the two sets of intentions, the two sets of signs, confront each other in hostility, then ethical space is set up instantaneously.

The space in the Prague photograph is an achieved intentional structure, something held in place, something willed.

In the photograph of the Russian and Chinese border guards approaching each other over the frozen Ussuri River, the space is still to be established *as* Russian or *as* Chinese. It is as yet a space of contention, an inert lump of space upon which meaning has still to be conferred. Both the Russians and the Chinese make a claim to ownership, and their claim is mutually disallowed.

The Ussuri River is not yet owned in the sense in which the Prague park was owned. But ethical space is set up immediately. There is no action which could be undertaken in that area of ice which would not immediately be interpreted and invested with an ethical and political significance.

Nevertheless, the actors in the drama on the ice are in possession of only half the evidence they need to interpret. There is as yet not access to the intentions of the others on the ice, as the body is being suspended, deliberately, as a signifier. Both sides are waiting for the signs to begin, but neither has yet begun to emit any.

The actions awaited are about to make explicit all that is at the moment only potential.

Ethical space is set up, however, in a provisional and potential sense. Confrontation, encounter, two opposed sets of values — all these are in evidence as the figures move

across the ice. The solitude of the human being in that waste of ice is impressive. But so far the body has not been used.

Each of the three Russians and each of the three Chinese is alone, surrounded by that hostility, connected only tenuously to his companions and to his adversaries by these natural hazards and by the force of his diplomatic enterprise. Each individual is alone, but his role has been selected for him in advance.

Over the frozen river (itself a dubious asset and belonging to that tenuous class of objects which are desirable only because they are politically advantageous to another power) the Chinese and the Russians advance towards each other, cast in their roles which are known beforehand and which have depersonalized them into diplomatic non-entities.

Each of the six as he advances is carrying on a personal enterprise, however. Each is drawing on the slightest detail of the physical presence of the others which might enable him to construct, from the impassivity of the body withheld as a sign, some immediately usable grammar, in terms of which the ensuing actions can be judged, and to some extent presupposed or evaded.

The smallest detail is seized upon, in this pre-intentional time, which might help him in his interpretative task, which might allow him to comment upon it internally, to invest it with a provisional meaning, and therefore to be able to react appropriately when the time comes.

Since the bodies of the approaching three are impassive, suspended, held deliberately in a state of immobility which excludes the sign, what is searched for in this hostile encounter is a lead as to the probable intentions of the others. It is a task of visual speculation. The body is examined as a suspended sign.

The Russians, advancing across the ice preserved for us on this dim plate, recognize the Chinese as human beings like themselves, as possessed of feelings, hopes and fears like themselves, and try to set up a series of equivalences between the values of the Chinese and their own. *Mutatis mutandis* the Chinese do the same.

But everything else is provisional. They recognize, in the slow advance of their opponents across the ice, an unwilling servitude to political power structures which correspond to their own. They are conscious that their opponents must be feeling the cold, the pain, the hunger and the danger of fighting under these conditions as they themselves do. They suppose them to have families and friends.

But as the Chinese and Russians advance towards each other, these are all the clues that they can muster. For the other is still reserving his signs.

2

SUBJECTIVITY AS EXPRESSION IN THE WORLD

A fault has occurred in our reason. One half of our modern rationality has dropped sheerly away, leaving the cliff face of scientific and political objectivity towering uselessly over the void.

The strata of reason, thus violently sundered, continue at a lower level, but they are unrecognizable from above. Objectivity has been deserted, left high and exposed, by subjectivity.

This drop away from rational conformity has been given visually in a number of striking and original ways, some of which are now so familiar to us as to have been accepted as features of our world without having been examined for their meaning. We have grown familiar with the sign without ever taking seriously its signification.

The sign has been given visually in a whole variety of modulations and subdivisions. In all forms, however, subjectivity has used its physical presence in the world as a means of establishing its desire to sunder with accepted objectivity.

The body is the outward and visible form of subjective intention and meaning. It is the encoded form of a message constantly emitted over the last decade: the message that there has been a mutation in our sense of what is right and wrong. What was acceptable once is so no longer. Everything has to be thought out again.

The most striking form has been the international student movement, which is inflected in a double manner. It is evidently a resurgence of Romantic sentiment, and also a re-affirmation of moral values that can easily be likened to a new Reformation.

We have now come to associate the blue jeans, tasselled leather jerkins, broad belts, tinted sunglasses, crucifixes, bangles and baubles, earrings, Service overcoats and psychedelic scarves with a distinct class of non-assenting citizens, permanently visible in our society. The clothes code is of course a Romantic one, going back to Byron at least and descending through the dress vagaries of the *poète maudit* to the fopperies of the *décadence*. We have learnt that through the use of this code, every dress convention of bourgeois society is systematically inverted. We have grown accustomed to the fact that a very large section of young persons, students or others, have expressed a desire not to be integrated into our society, a desire which is kept constantly before our eyes as we walk along the streets.

Extending the clothes-code to the body itself, the Hippy sub-section of the student phenomenon has accustomed us to long hair and a disregard for personal cleanliness, both of which again testify to a distaste, deeply felt, for conformist social values. The bourgeois code is again systematically inverted: since well-dressed or short hair and a careful body hygiene are demanded by the middle conforming sections of society, the obvious thing to do, if one wishes to 'drop out', is to disregard these injunctions. Antipathy thus generated is a useful pointing up of the differences of credo between the two groups.

All this is by now well known, even commonplace. But the signification of these signs is still systematically disregarded: no attempt is made to heal the breach.

Other Romantic structures of the student movement are perhaps less obvious, though just as striking, as the clothes-body code. There is the immense desire for transcendence, for a better, ideal world, which is indistinguishable as a form from that passionate Romantic *essor* which is given perfect pictorial expression in, say, John Martin's fantasy-picture 'Manfred on the Jungfrau'. There, the immense hazy distances, the precipices and valleys sweep up in a kind of frenzy of excitement towards the limitless heavens, in a passionate affirmation that the soul of man and the divine are one and the same thing in their striving to transcend the restrictions of matter and time. 'The Plains of Heaven' by the same painter expresses the Romantic love of the hazy, the far-away and the ethereal, a mood given, in a more historical manner, in the inspired imprecisions of, say, Turner's 'Childe Harold's Pilgrimage in Italy'.

The modern equivalents of this mood and desire are easy to discern in the young Romantics. First meditation and then drugs were adopted as means to transcendence. The emphasis on the aesthetic and the sensual in this transcendence (it was a desire of the original Romantic aesthetic to involve *all* the senses at once) is also very pronounced. Human beauty and the enjoyment thereof can itself be used as a means of transcendence. All the senses are involved, the painfulness of the mind is allayed.

The new Romanticism looks to Nature for a solution of the problems of modern social living. The negligent personal dress and toilet is part of the indifference felt for the ethos of the drawing-room, but much more positive feelings of dependence on Nature are in evidence. The retreat to Nature implies the adoption of heroes and heroines who in a high degree symbolize the instinctual life. It implies the adoption of natural divinities, spirits of the earth, the forest and the plain. Thus Che Guevara and Fidel Castro are heroes partly at least because they haunt the forest in their fight against the town and all the bureaucratic corruption the town implies. The Maharishi inhabits the mountains and plains of mysterious India, immortal land. Folk-heroes like the Easy Rider come into being: the Easy Rider who, Hippy and drug-taker, sets out across the open countryside in a search for the sources of the natural life of mountain, hill and plain. Twice the Easy Rider is tempted to break off his search: once with the farmer on his wide fertile acres and once with the nomad community which plants its seed with an ardent prayer for fruition and for peace. The Easy Rider represents that search, for a return to the 'source' of natural living, which has been given philosophic expression by Heidegger in his idea of *Gelassenheit** and by Marcuse in his doctrine of a retreat from the iron kingdom of necessity to the realm of universal Eros.

The retreat to nature and the natural values of unaffected pre-social man is impregnated with the spirit of Rousseau as well as of modern Romantic philosophers like Heidegger and Marcuse. The modern Romantics revert to a primitive model of society where lands and goods would be held in a kind of benevolent elemental communism. Rousseau wrote:

The first man who, having staked off a bit of land, said, 'This is mine', and found people stupid enough to believe him, was the true founder of civil society. How many crimes, wars, murders, how many miseries and horrors someone would have

* Martin Heidegger, *Discourse on Thinking*, Harper & Row, New York, 1966, p. 54.

spared mankind who, uprooting the stakes or shovelling in the ditch, had called to his fellows: 'Don't listen to the liar! You are lost if you forget that the fruits of the earth belong to all of us, the land to no-one'.*

The new Romantics hold to this communist Rousseau-ism passionately. The device of the sit-in, the invasion of administrative offices, the occupying of deserted buildings or the sequestration of occupied buildings, have become familiar tropes in the Romantic discourse. The milieu which is seized is asserted to belong to all. A kind of primitive tribal life is instituted, where goods, food and women are held in common, as in the Sorbonne and the Odéon in May 1968. This provocation sets off a real aggression in the legal owners, who call in the police and eject the sitters from their property by force. The owners are thus provoked into asserting their property-rights, which are precisely what the sitters most object to. The more violent the ejection the more unnatural does the fact of ownership appear to be.

Another form of the retreat to Nature appears clearly in the trope of the walking hieroglyph. Language is suspect because it has to do with bureaucracy, exploitation, and unfairness of every kind, unfairness associated with a progressive distortion of all true natural (i.e. pre-literate) values. Language thus being near allied to the forms of political and bureaucratic tyranny and impersonality, the young Romantics will have none of it, preferring silence or a minimum of symbolic utterance which is itself coded: 'You see, man, it's like this, man ...' etc., where the appeal is explicitly made to that understanding which can occur on the natural, human, pre-verbal level.

This doctrine too can be found clearly expressed in Rousseau; 'These three manners of writing correspond

* *De l'inégalité parmi les hommes*, pt ii.

pretty exactly to the three kinds of society in which one can observe men living together. Picture-language (hieroglyphs) is suitable to wild peoples; signs of words and propositions (ideograms) are suitable to barbarian peoples; and the alphabet is suitable to people living in a policed state.'* The whole doctrine of language expressed by Rousseau in the *Essay on the Origin of Languages* is believed in implicitly (if unconsciously) by the walking hieroglyphs.

Indeed the wild poetry of the Hippy language is a deliberate return to that language of tropes which Rousseau asserted to be the beginning of language in a state of nature. Developing in a kind of rapid cross-fire their own language of freshly hewn myth and irreverent parody, the Romantics wage war against the accepted verbal traditions of the *status quo* with creative insouciance. At the recent Chicago 'conspiracy trial', the prosecution spoke in prose, the defendants in verse. There could be no more vivid demonstration of the fundamental political opposition which was there under debate. Rousseau again: 'Figurative language was the first to be born, the language of sense last.... First of all, only poetry was spoken, reasoning came a long time after.'

Rousseau's theory is astonishingly close to what appears to be the theoretical infrastructure of the beliefs of the modern Romantics. According to Rousseau, the original language of men would have been a series of tropes, of appeals from one man to another, a series of calls, images or metaphors.

Only in the formalization of these elementary human linguistic particles came that hierarchization and formalization which splits men up into owners and owned, educated and uneducated, rich and poor, powerful or helpless. At that moment the primal *pitié* which originally existed

* *Essai sur l'origine des langues*, chapter 5.

between men gave way to hatred, inequality and exploitation. The scribal class begins to exploit the unlettered and the possession of language and of culture becomes a powerful means of enforcing and maintaining a *status quo*. All education (and with it all advancement up the social ladder) is held by the Church, the scribes and the bureaucrats educated by them. With formalized written language, the age of misery begins for man, and the police state can be instituted. A call-up card is signed by no-one.

Language is thus the ladder to social and economic advancement. It is when the theme becomes specifically economic that the subjective opposition of the young Romantics emerges as overt hostility to the *status quo*.

It is a characteristic of all primitive romanticism, in any age, to despise money as such, *a priori*. Rousseau insisted, in the *Contract*, on the evils of money. And since advancement in the bureaucratic or economic system is a prize awarded to the adept manipulator of words, the Romantics have a double reason for refusing to play the game.

In rejecting language, the Romantics reject with it all the struggle, the panting and pushing, which the modern meritocracy of competence and 'drive' demands. Where the bourgeois (industrialist, politician, businessman, academic) utters his thoughts in an uninterrupted flow, articulating clearly and as far as possible grammatically, inflecting his tone and cadences in accordance with the accepted manner of that sub-group in society he belongs to (or wants to belong to), the young Romantic will refuse to speak at all, or else adopt a kind of rhapsodic utterance, innocent of structure or grammar, and in which questions are not cast in an interrogative form. Language will be reduced again to tropes.

This attitude to the economic substructure of industrial society represents a split in its own rationality. Because the 'system' is literate, the Romantic regards reading and writing with suspicion, and takes a pride in the small amount of books that have come under his purview or in the small amount of analysis he has brought to bear upon them. He is not interested in education in the old sense, nor in 'getting on' in the world. Because competence (success in the world of business and of money) is a bourgeois value only attainable through the word and literacy, the Romantic settles down comfortably into a willed and accepted mediocrity. The academic, too complicit in Culture, becomes suspect. The treatment meted out to Paul Ricoeur as Dean of Nanterre is significant in this respect. The demagogue of the extreme Left finds fertile ground to throw his seed upon. The university becomes a natural domain and a generalized Romanticism lulls the collective campus unconscious into a pastoral mood. But it is only implicitly Romanticism in Rousseau's sense: more explicitly it will be the Romanticism and the idealism of Mao which exerts the more positive enchantment.

Rousseau: 'In a genuinely free country, the citizens do all with their strong right arms, nothing with their money.' The young Romantics claim that the economic structure of their society is rotten, evil. The industrial society in which we live cannot understand this downgrading to contempt of its most cherished value. Neither the pillars of industry nor the young Romantics who refuse to integrate into industry have read Rousseau's *Contrat Social*. But the subjective opposition of the Romantics, given in a poverty and a disregard for personal possessions and personal prestige worthy of the begging friars of earlier days, has had its effect. Industrial society has had to take account of the massed hostility of the younger generation to those values accepted as unquestionable by itself and by its parents and grandparents.

One of the major issues in the subjective rebellion against objectivity is thus economic, purely. It is the issue of the status of money as such. The 'events of May' in France in 1968 brought this dissatisfaction with money directly into prominence.

The French students had a double quarrel with the economic structure of their society. On a personal level the students felt a grudge against the academic system which was turning them out *'bons pour le chômage'*, ready for unemployment. They claimed to have been educated in such a way that they now had ample provision of unteachable information, or qualifications for non-existent jobs.

But the much deeper dissatisfaction was shown to be with the economic structure of French society itself. The structure of that society being industrial and capitalist, the students had moral qualms about being integrated into it at all. They were opposed to eventual integration into a capitalist society which they hated. It was in this that the events of May took on their ideological significance for students all over the world.

Subjective dissatisfaction thus found its expression in the heady street-skirmishes of May. These 'events' shook French society to its foundations, and nearly unseated General de Gaulle. There is no question but that the much-despised *groupuscules* had, in their physical deployment in the streets and squares of Paris, made a criticism of French society that that society was forced to consider.

This physical deployment in the streets is a method of provocation which was brought to a fine art in the 1960s. A moral question is *physically* posed in a march, sit-in, or confrontation with the police. The provocation consists in getting the system (whichever it be) to show itself in its true colours, to show the world whether there is any moral force, any chain of reasoning which can justify itself explicitly, behind the constant stream of directives and prohibitions emitted.

When the police are called in, as they were in California, Madrid, Berlin, Prague and Paris, the provocation works beautifully. Brute force does indeed appear to be all that lies behind the moral façades of the system, which is seen to be morally and intellectually bankrupt when violent retaliation is always and inevitably substituted for reasoned self-defence or explanation of its policies.

As embodied subjectivities, the protest marchers and sitters-in of the 1960s have mounted a series of moral questions in visual form. By denying the validity of what is the case, and implicitly suggesting the desirability of what is not the case, a series of indirect communications have in fact been filtered from one section of rationality to the other.

However, a carefully preserved insensitivity to the visual message, together with an ever-increasing swing to the Right in political feeling all over the world, have succeeded in blocking access to that privileged neutral area where what was offered as implicit moral criticism could be taken up and discussed as explicit ethical problem. The indirect communications of the 1960s seem to have achieved the opposite result to what was obviously intended. But that makes the fault in our reason even more sinister than it was before.

The protest march, a traditional form of communication after all, took on a new importance in the 1960s because of its new semantic ingredient: its disinterested idealism. The march was not for immediate personal gain but for peace and harmony of nations. The evident moral conce 1 of those who felt it worth their while to march in the days of the Campaign for Nuclear Disarmament rallies in Trafalgar Square and elsewhere had its effect. The effect was so strong because a new message was enclosed in the old sign.

As the decade progressed, the motivations of the marches became more varied. There was concern, not only about the proliferation of nuclear arms, but also about weapons of biological warfare and about the university research which produced them. Vietnam, South Africa and Greece all had their repercussions in the streets and on the campuses. The climax came in 1968, in Paris and Czechoslovakia. This was the high moment of the body as sign.

Very like young Luthers, the young Romantics impugn the old order and its double standards of morality. The new Romantic consciousness, in its fundamental challenge to the accepted moral code of our day, might very well be seen as the most significant deepening of ethical consciousness since the Reformation.

Luther objected to the fact that the money being taken from the credulous for indulgences was being sent to raise the most magnificent monument to human pride in the world: St Peter's Church in Rome. The young Romantics feel that the world's wealth would be better spent on the relief of famine and disease than on the nuclear arms race or the space race.

Luther insisted upon the validity of the individual conscience and personal conviction, denying the supremacy of human authority in matters concerning the individual conscience. The Romantics demand the cessation of moral intimidation, and demand a classless world of free individuals bowed down under no authority which is external to man's own moral sense of how things should be.

Luther attacked corruption and the abuses of the church system, laziness and crassness of spiritual life, all short cuts to salvation or advancement which did not pass through the narrow defile of individual effort. The Romantics substitute the spirit of the law for its letter and seek for the moral law within themselves.

A new Reformation. Only, in the 1960s, it was not led by a single monk, hiding in retreat in Saxony, but by an entire level of international consciousness as such.

This rebellion against accepted authority, this assertion of the validity of the individual will over the law, is not only a deepening of Protestant consciousness (the spirit of Protestantism and not its dogma) but also, of course, a supremely Romantic gesture of isolation and defiance. It is, so to speak, the Romanticism of the Reformation. In the face of decisions made by impersonal authority, the individual elects himself supreme arbiter of what is right and wrong. The individual, in his Romantic guise, rebels against the reason and the morality of the *Ancien Régime* and makes a new Declaration of Independence.

The most striking feature of this complex phenomenon is, paradoxically, its mass nature. Millions of young individuals have felt sufficiently in agreement with one another on the major issues of our day for their individual protest to have taken on the character of a group expression. This is an old sign with a new content. The individual is supreme, and yet he chooses to express himself in a mass demonstration.

The only expressive tool which the international movement of feeling could immediately find and deploy was the body as sign of attack and defence. The use of the body as an intentional sign thus immediately took on an ideological importance. The Reformers had to choose a sign to express their convictions, and the body was peculiarly fitted to the task because of the many significant modes in which it could be utilized.

The rhetoric developed slowly. As obstacle, the body was used to block traffic and processions. As protest, it deployed on specific issues across streets or campus. Once possessed of the theoretical importance of the principles of Che Guevara and of Régis Debray, the Germans, the Japanese and the French developed these techniques of local harassment to a fine art, always fitting their attack to the terrain.

As sign, the body massed and marched, threw up barricades and attacked tanks with timber lances. As lived subjective reality, the body became the symbolic centre of aesthetic, sexual and religious cults, from the original San Francisco Hippies through *Hair* and *Woodstock* up to the Jesus Revolution. As a centre of freedom it undertook the new responsibility of the Odyssey of drugs. Drugs as *sign* represent the denial of the limits of experience as laid down by bourgeois society. Perhaps the spirit of that denial is best captured in the words that Dante gives Ulysses to speak in the Eighth Bolgia of his *Inferno*:

> *non vogliate negar l'esperïenza,*
> *di retro al sol, del mondo sanza gente.*
> *Considerate la vostra semenza:*
> *fatti non foste a viver come bruti,*
> *ma per seguir virtute e canoscenza.* *

These stirring words to his oarsmen express Ulysses' burning desire to press on and out, beyond the known and permitted limits of experience.

The body of the young Romantic becomes a walking sign of negation and refusal. Dress, toilet, sexual, religious

---

* Do not choose to deny the experience of the world without people behind the sun. Consider the seed from which you spring: you were not born to live like brutes, but to follow virtue and knowledge.

and social conventions of bourgeois society are all systematically overturned through the symbolism of the
body. Even the inherited limits of the *mind* are rejected
through the same corporal symbolism, through the drug
experience. The mind now admits no limits: it has become the body. Everything that the cultural and intellectual bourgeois society had shored up against its ruin was
rejected. That society has not, even yet, understood or
accepted the depth and violence of that rejection.

But the body was capable of a communication which
transcended all of these. And that communication was
made possible by the subjective presence in the world of
Mr Dubček in Czechoslovakia.

For it is striking that the passion for individual freedom
and choice which we have called Romantic is not confined to the West, nor even to a specific generation.
Romanticism is an ever-open possibility to the human
spirit, in all places and across all generations. Behind the
Iron Curtain, a period of relative thaw allowed of a variety
of Romantic assertions, communications directed towards
the centralized control of Soviet Russia. The revolt of the
Czechs stands out perhaps most clearly as an example.

Dubček led a movement of consciousness which would
have carried Czechoslovakia to a quite new freedom and
independence if that effort had not been curtailed in the
brutal way we witnessed. Only gradually did the importance of Dubček's indirect communication become present
to the Czech people. It was as if he was working from
within, modifying their ideas about what was permissible
and what was possible. By his appearance, his work, his
significant interventions, Dubček powerfully worked on
the moral sense of his compatriots. At the moment of
crisis, the indirect communicator, who has prepared his
communication carefully over a long period of time, sud-

denly emerges as a symbolic figure in his true historical meaning. Suddenly he corresponds to a deep subjective need in his fellow-countrymen, and in an act of sudden insight, they *identify* him.

The photographs of the resistance to the Russian tanks that rolled into Prague provided eloquent testimony to the level of protest involved. Suddenly the process towards freedom is halted and the act supervenes. The history of consciousness is again brought to a halt.

Dubček was never allowed after those weeks to speak in his own defence, but was submitted to one humiliation and degradation after another. But with every stripping away of honour and position, his communication acquired new depth and meaning. Silence in Dubček became so powerful a visual sign that no amount of words flowing the other way against him could have the slightest effect upon his Czech counter-subjects.

It is in the subjective context established by Mr Dubček that the apotheosis of the communication of the body is reached. It is the communication of Jan Palach. The body used in *that* peremptory manner, as a simple incontrovertible sign of negation and refusal, is absolutely shocking in its subjective effect. In that sign meet three extremes of assertion: extreme Romanticism, extreme ethical conviction, and extreme subjectivity. There is no answer to the communication of Jan Palach. The statement is final and absolute.

Palach made a many-layered assertion in his act. Apart from the political significance which his act has in the specific historical setting of Prague, his act establishes a whole network of validities for the body as sign.

The body is established as the final, and perhaps only, dense secure moral value in our world. Nothing else is shared as surely as it. In extreme situations, the body alone is left to signify with. When the situation makes verbal statement impossible or robs it of any meaning, the body can be used as ultimate *non placet*.

The body is established as the locus of all ethical experience. Nothing happens to me which does not happen to my body. Insult the body and you insult the freedom within it. Attack the body, you attack the person. Torture the body, you mutilate the individual. Kill the body and you kill the spirit which inhabits it. For we are never in doubt as to where to place the wreath. The value has spoken and the body is dead. But with a sure hand we lay the wreath on the body itself, last shred and remnant of the spirit which worked with such powerful indirect effect in the world.

The body is the locus of all ethical experience, and all experience is, because spatial, ethical. There can be no act which does not take place in ethical space. There can be no 'flaccid' act, no act devoid of all significance, no unconditioned act.

The meaning conferred upon the act will of course be a function of the perspective from which it is seen and of the moral presuppositions which the viewer brings to bear. A meaning will thus be conferred, instantaneously, on any act in space, and this meaning is therefore inevitably an ethical one.

Palach invests the body with significance by destroying it in what is given as public space. But then the body destroyed is an ethical body (is instinct with ethical significance) because all public space is by definition ethical space. In this way, Palach concatenates the inner world of values and the outer world of experience, the world of necessity and the world of chance, by translating a physical object directly into a spiritual value.

It is in this manner, at least, that his death is received and understood in Prague.

Probably one has to go back as far as Fichte to find a sufficiently powerful theory of the body as ethical signifier. In *The Science of Rights* (1796) we read:

> The will of the person enters the sensuous world only insofar as it is expressed in the determination of the body. In this sphere of the sensuous world the body itself of a free being is, therefore, to be regarded as itself the final ground of its own determination; and the free being, as appearance is here identical with its body. The body is the representative of the Ego in the sensuous world, and where the sensuous world alone enters into consideration, the body itself is the Ego. Hence we use every day such phrases as '*I* was not there', 'He has seen *me*', '*He* is born, *he* died, *he* was buried', etc.*

Fichte asserts that it is only in the form of his body, his *eigenes Leib*, that we meet, interpret and understand the other. His body is the matrix of his rights and of his ethical will in the world, and also represents the physical limit of my own freedom in the world. Where his body begins the realm of my own moral autonomy ends. *He is* that limit. At the same time his body is the external form of his own freedom to signify his intentions in the world. In the face of this complex embodied phenomenon there can be, Fichte asserts, properly and adequately understood, only one correct attitude and it is the one which he enjoins upon us: absolute and unconditional respect.

For Fichte there can be no consciousness outside the realm of what he calls, following Kant, the practical reason. A moral vision of the world is inevitable: a moral vision of the world is quite simply our perception of the world itself. In that vision, the bodies of others necessarily

* Routledge & Kegan Paul, 1970, pp. 162-3.

form moral phenomena. Palach gave this fact shocking and unforgettable form.

In Russia itself, the subjective refusal of the objectivity which was responsible for the invasion of Czechoslovakia has been led, not by students, but by scientists and artists of the highest distinction. The more rigorous a political orthodoxy is, the higher have its critics to be in the scientific or social scale to challenge it effectively. Indeed it would seem that it is at the level of the Nobel prize that Russian subjectivity first gets an opportunity to wage its battle, at that moment when the criteria of the outside world have forced objectivity to take account of its critic.

The example of Boris Pasternak was striking enough. His communication consisted in declining the Nobel prize rather than abandoning his country. More recently, Alexander Solzhenitsyn chose not to receive the prize in Stockholm. Yevgeny Yevtushenko led a strong wave of feeling in publishing and reading *Babi Yar* – a feeling that was struggling to achieve a new freedom from racial prejudice. Yevtushenko emerged for a time as a genuine force in Russian culture, but the attempt to do what he did in the days after Kruschev led Daniel, Siniavsky and Amalrik to the provincial lagers. Those who speak up for Solzhenitsyn, as Rostropovitch did, are denied their permits to travel.

It is not surprising that subjective dissatisfaction should be expressed first by writers and musicians. But the split (the fault) in Russian objectivity appears clearly for what it is when leading Soviet scientists, in the interests of the very objectivity of their disciplines, add their weight to the subjective moment of unrest and critique. Only the most distinguished scientists, men like Academician Sakharov, can get a hearing, and his efforts were followed by the inevitable series of punitive restrictions on his work.

Towards Deep Subjectivity

The effort of certain Russian academics to set up a Human Rights Committee can scarcely expect more than stonewalling from Soviet authority. All these efforts are doomed to a short-term failure. Nevertheless the presence of a subjective critique at the very centre of Russian objectivity counts, it counts very strongly, in the eyes of the world, as a new possibility of freedom and humanity in the Soviet Union.

The Russian situation is significant, in that it indicates that it is precisely at the level of science (and an adequate philosophy of science) that subjective thinking has most to do at the moment. It is *there* that it has to make its start. It cannot begin straight away with political objectivity as such, but scientific internationalism and human feeling which leads to the creation of a Human Rights Committee and makes large protective gestures on behalf of writers and thinkers, will necessarily bring a saner and more human politics in their wake.

The large underground movement reporting on and circulating the results of private Soviet trials (like that of Amalrik) is another symptom of a felt split in the reigning objectivity in Russia. Scientists and artists are struggling to humanize Russian politics and to make artistic efforts and scientific research serve the ends of humanity rather than those of the Party. Whether they will succeed, after Budapest and Prague, remains to be seen – and yet this attack upon the reigning objectivity in Russia argues powerfully for the existence there of a committed and hostile subjectivity, fighting for the amelioration of the present system.

Russian subjectivity deploys its subjective presence in the world as a kind of sign of negation and dissatisfaction. This sign gains its emphasis and power from the deliberate self-exposure of the individual to the vengeance of the system. It is a kind of martyrdom freely offered in the service of a value held to be higher than those which are in evidence.

The eminence of the person himself (as scientist or artist) is held up against the practice of the system, as a kind of postulation of Romantic individualism over against technocratic totalitarianism. The sign thus carries a double potentiation: it is the affirmation of the distinguished over against the impersonal (unknown, mediocre), and it is the affirmation of the helpless over against the powerful.

Operating at the intellectual level, this sign demands an inquiry into *the distance between* the two values which thus lock in opposition. The sign is a subjective appeal for a certain *difference* to be noted, an *interval* between one thing and another, a *disproportion* asserted between what is and what should be. The sign thus deployed is conscious of posing a set of alternatives to the viewers in the world. This kind of indirect communication practised by the eminent Russian subjectivists is highly conscious of itself as a communication, and has as its explicit purpose the posing of a necessary *choice*.

In the foregoing examples, the body is quite evidently the matrix of significant expression. The body's signs are signifiers and the inner world of intention is the signified. In interpreting the signs we work back from the sign to the inner intention which animates them. The body when used expressively is a pure sign and a reliable access to the originating subjectivity offered through it.

But we have to deepen our understanding of bodily action. What of violent action, bomb-throwing, street-fights, armed hijacking and armed kidnapping? The person who carries out these acts is not offering his body as a communication. There is no doubt a very powerful subjectivity involved, lying behind these acts of aggression, but these acts are not offered as signs. They are in fact indexes. If the characteristic of a sign is that it intends to communicate something, then the characteristic of the index is that it is significant of something without having been emitted explicitly as a message. Terrorist acts, for example, while they may well have an explanation, even perhaps a justification, are not intended to signify, although they must obviously be significant of something. But attempting to understand the index is very different from interpreting the sign.

In a street-fight, a bomb-throwing, a riot with broken windows, thrown stones, tear gas and all the modern equipment of street warfare, the body of the aggressor, like that of the defendant, is incapable of interpretation. The body has no signified, because it is given as pure act. Violent action is not a message, and therefore violent action passes beyond the competence of interpretation. In violent action, the signifier corresponds to no signified. The violence may be explicable in many ways but it is not itself an offer of explanation. Violence practised for itself is visible but not operative as visual. It increases the distance to a possible signified to infinity and wishes to remain closed to all comprehension. The body in its terrorist usage is an index of pure non-expressivity.

Indeed the terrorist very often has no use at all for the body as intentional sign. Most often his activities are secret and he is personally absent from the scene of his protest. His bomb goes off hours after he has left the scene. It is in this kind of perspective that the total difference of the Romantic passive subjectivity which operates the body as sign, and the new terrorist subjectivity which deletes the body from its activities and aims at the destruction of existing meanings, most clearly emerges.

Subjectivity as Expression in the World

The structures of bodily expressivity, the deployed use of the sign, are lost in the world of the index. The development of Romantic student protest into the current forms of organized yet random violence operated by hard-core pressure groups, like the Weathermen in America, perfectly demonstrates the transition, not only historically but conceptually, from the sign to the index. And since the index is more and more attracting the attention of those concerned with the maintenance of law and order in the Western world, it is perhaps as well to distinguish the practitioners of the index from the practitioners of the sign.

In the 1960s, up to and including the Prague and Paris 'revolutions' of 1968, the Romantic cause was informed with the reformation of society, and used certain elementary techniques like the march and the sit-in and the street-blockage as signs in order to bring society to a clear recognition of its own moral plight. The use of the body was significant and intended to be so.

Even before 1968, there had been several observable variations of intention in the Romantic practice. That practice had opened peacably, it was highly idealistic, calling for 'dialogue', 'participation' and 'communication'. These calls were ignored, and the attitude of the Romantics hardened. The protest-marches on political issues began to incorporate several devices for provoking the agents of law and order to actions which could be read off as significant of the powers they served. Protest-marches gradually became confrontations, and a mutual tolerance between police and demonstrators turned by degrees into hostility. In England, an early climax in this hostility was reached in the Grosvenor Square incident, and in America the high point (the high visual point) is obviously the affair of Kent State University. Paris had its own show-down in 1968.

But even in the Paris of May 1968, the index began to merge into the activities of the sign. No doubt the street-skirmishes and barricades of May were devices of a powerful subjective reality which expressed itself in signs, but even before May was out, the Katangais were infesting the cellars of the Sorbonne and the Théâtre de l'Odéon. The terrorists emerged from the movement of May, and in America they were not long behind.

The emergence of the terrorists from the ranks of the young Romantics dealt a death-blow to the communicational techniques of the marches and sit-ins. These became suddenly useless as signs, for peaceful protest could suddenly be treated as being co-extensive with terrorist attacks upon the safety and continued existence of the body politic. A sit-in, a march, like the famous one at Kent State, could be treated as being the same (to all intents and purposes) as those violent acts practised by the terrorists. In fact, since 1968 we have watched the body-sign of the Romantics being progressively reduced to impotence by the introduction of the terrorist index.

From the moment when the traditional means of using the body as obstacle and as sign was taken from it by the activities of the terrorists, the Romantic cause subsided into ideological helplessness. The Romantic consciousness lost its pre-eminence as moral arbiter in its society, and has not yet recovered it. Indeed, it is difficult to see how, in the accelerating violence of a world in disintegration, that pre-eminence, or even a signifying competence, can be regained.

Events since 1968 have moved fast. Terrorist practices have outrun consciousness. The hard-core terrorists who emerged from the original Romantic protest do not share the consciousness of the Romantics. Their aims are different. They do not intend to parley with society, nor to help reform it, but to bring it crashing down by any means, fair or foul.

In America, this realization was the justification for a massive counter-attack. There was a historical change in the nature of consciousness which was made evident to every observer in the hardening of police action on the campuses. As that police action changed, so the protest became ever more intransigent. This marked the end of the original communication project of the Romantics. A front-page photograph in the *Guardian* in February 1971 showed Parisian students sitting-down in protest against the maiming of one of their fellows, and it is significant that every student is wearing a crash-helmet. In this way, the end of the reign of the sign in its first phase is visually proved.

The original sign has got swamped in a new set of indexes. That these indexes refer, at some deep level, to the same philosophy of rejection and despair held by the original Romantics may be true. But that there is a common source of meaning at the bottom of the signs and of the indexes does not imply that there is any longer a visual meaning offered at the level of the code. The Weathermen, to take an outstanding example, would be the first to deny the existence of that sort of coded meaning in their acts. Their aim is not to communicate something, not to reform something, it is not the emitting of messages that is in question. It amounts rather more to a declaration of war, a war to the death, in which struggle the values which imply 'dialogue', 'communication' and 'reform' (the slogans of the original movement) are of supreme irrelevance.

The bombings and riots which replace the original protest marches represent a conscious *substitution* of the index for the sign. It is taken as a premise that Western industrial society is incapable of reform, and the conclusion is drawn that the simple destruction of that society is a self-evidently justified aim. No further reflection seems to be expected by the terrorists on this point. To discuss what should be done when society has been brought down in ruins is considered merely reactionary. Consequently, the acts of the terrorists are not counters in an argument, but an outright refusal of discussion and gradual reform.

This aim, clear as it may be, is intentionally not a communicational one. The desire to change the existing system has given way to a desire to cripple it. With this change in the nature of the intentions involved goes the necessary change from expressivity to meaninglessness.

We thus have to deal with two overlapping subjectivities. It is sometimes very difficult to distinguish one from the other. For what is common to both is the total refusal of what is normally referred to as objectivity, reason, rationality and the discussion of aims and objectives that this implies. The Romantics have turned away from language in haughty disgust, and the terrorists are trying to abrogate it, beginning at the level of the destruction of the sign. It is not easy, though, to draw up the line of demarcation, because the subjectivity involved is in both cases profoundly opposed to the prevailing objectivity, whether this objectivity be political or philosophical or economic.

What we have watched through the course of the 1960s is the emergence of one sort of subjectivity from another. One might call it an intensification of subjectivity. The original Romantic subjectivity, inflected as it was with dreams and aspirations of the ideal, was of course opposed to the existing society on subjective grounds, but it included within itself a willingness to offer a directed and specific critique of society so that discussion could follow and better objective conditions be established.

But from the centre of this semantically potent subjectivity grew another, terrorist subjectivity. The major characteristic of this kind of subjectivity is the belief that no amount of talk will do any good. And consequently, the intention to be *subjectivist* at all levels and on all issues, the refusal to reason or to be reasoned with, the refusal to admit even the possibility of amelioration in objective conditions, amounts to a take-over bid for the world which expresses itself as a refusal of rationality in all its forms and a refusal to communicate visually as well as verbally.

It is difficult to draw up the lines of demarcation between these two subjectivities, and the great danger is that administrative repression (on both sides of the Iron Curtain, and in Europe as well as in America) will simply refuse to make the effort. The administration can now regard *all* protest, of every different kind, as being cut out of the same terrorist cloth. Conflating all brands of protest, even the individual one of a Rudi Dutschke or a Dubček, it feels fully justified in a full counter-offensive against all 'enemies of society'. A wholesale retaliatory exercise can now be mounted against all non-conformism. The dangers implicit in this are obvious.

The *status quo* can now (justifiably in its own eyes) weigh in with its heaviest instruments of repression. Instead of having to deal with an expressed and evident good-will in the signs of the body, it can treat all protest as emanating from 'radicals', 'university bums', 'Maoists', 'anarchists' and a whole array of social drop-outs, who have themselves dropped out, if they have, for very different reasons.

Among those drop-outs might be, for instance, those

who try to escape the draft for a war they consider immoral. But that refusal to be drafted, which originally belonged to the area of the sign, has been reduced, in a terrible refusal of semantic distinctions, to a mere index and is now accordingly punished with the rigour which is reserved for the suppression of the terrorists. This is the thin end of the wedge. It constitutes a danger to Romantic expressivity so great as to amount to a declared intention to annihilate the possibility of all signs.

The movement from the sign to the index implies an annihilation of ethical space, an attack upon the semantic properties of space. This movement of sudden and random violence carries with it the movement from original natural occupancy of the world into a world of terror and uncertainty, which affects everyone and the entire subjective climate.

One of the main reasons for the terror is the feeling that the possibility of rational discussion, of objective discourse, has been lost. The movement from the sign to the index marks the falling away from the area in which things can be discussed, from the world of dialogue, of rationality, of valid personal effort, of personal safety and of a logical and unbroken connection between this world and the world coming into existence. When diplomats are kidnapped and murdered as a mere bagatelle then no man, woman or child can rely on his personal safety being regarded as humanly (that is to say, semantically) significant. The movement from sign to index marks not only the perpetual impossibility of a solution to the problems we face, but also a perpetual refusal of discussion about them. The fall away from the sign and from objectivity held up as an ideal implies the fall away from any discussable solution to any dilemma whatsoever, and this increases a feeling of terror generated by acts which refuse to operate within the traditional limits and conventions of the body as sign.

Most seriously of all, the adoption of terrorist subjectivity, of violence in general, of that savage indifference to fellow human-beings which is being engendered through the constant exposure to such events as the Vietnam War, means that the ethical world is put into abeyance. The ethical space in which we lived until now is in process of being suspended.

In the new sort of space set up by terrorists, kidnappers, hi-jackers and bomb-throwers, space loses its ethical and intentional meaning. If a bomb goes off in an airport, an office building, a library, under a bridge or in a bank, it is anybody's guess who will be hurt. It is not even *probably* going to be a police officer, a judge or some significant figure in the hierarchy of political power. It is some innocent members of the public who will be mutilated, some private individuals in an aeroplane who will be shot, some wife or mother who will take the brunt of the attack. To this dehumanization of ethical space, the terrorists have no attitude at all. It is a matter of indifference who in particular is hurt in the explosion or shot in the kidnapping. The main aim being to terrorize and paralyse the system, or to hold it to ransom, the question of who gets mutilated or destroyed in the process is immaterial. The end justifies the means, and in the process space is robbed of any meaning at all.

This process can be seen most clearly in Northern Ireland. The first resurgence of the problem was expressed in symbolic acts and directed attacks. As time went on, and the situation was allowed to degenerate, violence became more random. On 25 August 1971 a bomb went off in the Belfast offices of the Northern Ireland Electricity Board, killing one person and wounding 35 others. The

Guardian photograph for the 26th shows shocked and bleeding office girls huddled in an ambulance. This opened a new phase in the violence. On 2 September three bombs went off in the city centre of Belfast. The *Guardian* for the 3rd wrote: 'No warning calls were received before the bombs exploded in buildings. They were timed to go off when streets and offices were likely to be filled with people on their way to lunch. More than 40 people were taken to hospital after the blasts ... People stood in knots, some of them weeping with fear in the pouring rain.' The bombs do not go off in *significant* places, but 'in buildings', in streets, offices and car-parks. Neither does the use of bombs *signify* anything: they are merely used to provoke random terror in the civilian population.

Meanwhile, soldiers are gunned down from passing cars, shot in the back by snipers, shot even when in civilian clothes and off duty. These acts, however costly in human terms, remain mere indexes. The agent is anonymous, he does not appear, his body is never in evidence, and so the drift towards the destruction of meaning gathers force.

And the result is that more and more people, when interviewed, express themselves as unable to *think the situation through*. They are unable to *think* what the outcome can be, they can *see* no solution. The situation has become literally un-thinkable. The destruction of ethical space is itself the destruction of the very possibility of thought.

It is evident from this that the careful placing and investment of body-signs in space as carried out by the original Romantics has been superseded and annulled by this new violence.

The terrorist attempt to deprive space of its ethical significance, to deprive the body of its semantic function as sign and symbol, of its meaningful disposition in space, is in fact an attack upon human reason itself. It becomes impossible to *think* under the new spatial conditions. It is no longer possible to judge, to make comparisons and to draw conclusions from the signs, because the signs have been abrogated and annulled. What we see is getting progressively harder to analyse. Terrorism aims at destroying all coherent visual structures, and through this succeeds in destroying all objectivity and all reason as such. It is a terrifying achievement.

Two sorts of subjectivity in the world, as different from each other in aims and significance as it is possible to imagine, have been contrasted in the preceding pages. Subjectivity is common to both, but one sort of subjectivity has been shown to be working for betterment of objective conditions and the other has been shown to be intent upon destroying them without parley. The structures of these two sorts of subjectivity have been only lightly sketched in. There is an immense amount more that needs to be said to distinguish the two sorts of subjectivity adequately.

But the fact that they have in common this massive hostility to received objectivity should cause some qualms. What is it about objectivity (political, scientific, social, ideological) which can raise such bitter resentment and hatred in such vast masses of people? For there is indeed a split in our reason, such that current objectivity no longer satisfies the demands being made upon it by people who, whatever their differences, have in common that they are not so hostile for nothing. They are not cretins. They have a point of view. What is it in objectivity, as subjectivity sees it, that so offends?

What, too, of the objectivity which we have (presumably) to defend? Is it objective enough? Part at least of the violence of the current situation can be attributed directly to the failure of objectivity to be fully objective, to take into account the needs and demands of subjectivity in the world. Unless, indeed, objectivity ceases to regard its criteria in the crabbed and formalistic manner that it has done up to now, there is a great likelihood that the whole of current objectivity will cave in under the attacks of the subjectivists. The American system, like the Russian one, seems likely to collapse from the bitter opposition felt within it, opposition which gnaws away at its rationality from within and opposes its aims in the world. Such a split rationality cannot survive long in the world, and cannot claim either, having left so much out of account, to be called objective.

One of the failures of objectivity leaps to the eye. There has been no *objective* reply (cast in terms of politics or ethics) to the questions posed through the 1950s and 1960s by subjective malcontents on both sides of the Iron Curtain. The questions posed in the indirect communications of the student movement, of Budapest and of Prague, have not been met or answered. Politicians have continued on their way under the influence of a certain *hubris*, which has as its form the belief that intensely unpopular actions need no sanction from the general public. No explanations for these actions and policies have been forthcoming, and it is quite clear why the resistance to authoritarian government has grown in intensity in the last decade. No viable philosophy has emerged in the West which could justify what is going on, or suggest an alternative set of beliefs and actions. In Russia, and its satellites, the official philosophy is not subject to questioning, either in theoretical or in practical terms. The minor 'philosophies' of *praxis* which have emerged from Cuba, Bolivia and China have therefore been snapped up eagerly. Better a destructive ethos of self-help and militancy than no ideological help at all.

Subjectivity as Expression in the World

It may be too late to resuscitate the idea of objectivity, *adequate* objectivity, in the West. We have sunk so deep into the facile objectivity of positivism in philosophy and behaviourism in psychology (both academic and applied) that it seems too late to modify what objectivity is before it sets hard as a political attitude of the Right and digs in its trenches for a prolonged war with subjectivity. It is difficult to see how objectivity can be taken out of the jealous guardianship of the politicians, the verificationists and the cynically self-interested.

But maybe there is still a moment left to re-define objectivity in such a way that it is enabled to take into account the new demands made upon it at the moment. Maybe there is still a moment to interrupt that process of willed deafness which is nearly total already. It lies, of course, with the defenders of objectivity to rescue it from that sterility in which it labours at the moment, in the last agony of a concern for method which dates from Bacon, Descartes, and Newton.

But objectivity of that kind, which attempts to exclude the thinker rigorously from the thought, has to bend to take account of the subjective challenge it has to deal with now. Without taking the fact of subjectivity into account, without inquiring into the possible validity of the reasons for subjectivity's total opposition to itself, without integrating the ideological factors of the subjective revolt into its analysis, objectivity's considerations are less than objective and its conclusions no conclusions at all.

3

'OBJECTIVITY'

'Objectivity'* is made up of a regress of tautologies. One of the definitions of a tautology offered by the *Shorter O.E.D.* is as follows: 'c. Applied to the repetition of a statement as its own reason, or to the identification of cause and effect.' It is in that sense of self-referring closedness towards external criteria that I use the word here.

Objectivity is what is commonly received as objectively valid, all the attitudes, presuppositions, unquestioned assumptions typical of any given society. Objectivity implies the acceptance of the dominant social, ethical and religious views in that society. Objectivity is, for all practical purposes, the totality of what is taken to be the case, believed to be the case, affirmed to be the case. Objectivity is the totality of received opinion on what is acceptable/not acceptable, desirable/not desirable, good/not good,

---

* The word is to be read in inverted commas throughout; what is in question is not adequate objectivity, achieved after an analysis which integrates the subjective into its result, but that impoverished fragment of human reason with which we are only too familiar.

etc. Objectivity in any given society in fact gets defined as the political and social *status quo*.

Objectivity is the belief in objectivity as such. By definition, objectivity is that which holds itself in place as the dominant and unquestioned objectivity of a given society.

Largely, the coincidence of the power *status quo* with the objective *status quo* is a matter of political *a priori*. Intellectual and political objectivity are always clamped together within the existing power structure. The facts which are recognized will be those which the powers that be recognize to be helpful to the prevailing political objectivity. This follows of itself. Hence, anyone who does not see the 'obvious' as the obvious will be taken to be suffering from delusions of one kind or another, to be suffering anyway from an impaired sense of objectivity. But as a sufferer from 'mere subjectivity' he can be safely ignored, or in certain countries he may eventually be handed over to a psychiatric hospital for treatment.

The *status quo* obtaining at any given moment is therefore the *status quo* only because there is a very harmonious fit between what is accepted as objective in politics and what is given out as objectivity in the universities and the press. If there were in fact any pressure for a change in the nature of objectivity, pressure felt among those who hold the *status quo* in place, objectivity would be redefined overnight.

Objectivity can then be defined in terms of itself, tautologically. The emergence of a thinker who does not see objectivity objectively, like Galileo or Chomsky, puts objectivity into danger. The tautology is destroyed. An element claiming to have a higher degree of objectivity than the received one is challenging it from within itself. It is at that moment that objectivity ceases to be an evident coincidence with itself.

There seem to be three major structures of objectivity. Others are in fact subdivisions of these. They are: a tenacious and unquestioning grasp of 'facts' (data, and the quantifiability of data); a refusal to make public the justification for its acts and decisions; and an inbuilt tendency to take account of the parts rather than the whole.

Objectivity contends that 'facts' have to be accepted if there is to be objective discourse. It is considered sub-rational to question the status of facts. In mathematics, physics, biology, chemistry, there are facts. It is therefore evident to objectivity that all human ratiocination which claims to be objective should adopt the impersonal stance of the scientist. Objectivity insists that facts have to be reckoned with and arranged in some convenient way. The suggestion that some facts ought not to be facts is rejected as merely subjective.

Objectivity insists that the facts be *accepted*. It takes as a premise that facts can be deployed in an objective, context-free way, even when the facts are about human beings. This insistence upon objectivity in facts concerning human life is what gives rise to the impersonal jargon of military strategy, where the tragic is buried under the official phrase. The facts of a situation have to be accepted for what they are: all subjective, ethical inquiry about the status of the facts under discussion is down-graded as sub-rational. An inquiry into facts which begins, like Chomsky's, by questioning the status of the facts themselves, when re-integrated into their human context, is simply disregarded as dangerous to objectivity.

Objectivity stands then for an acceptance of the facts and an exclusion of all affectivity from objective argument. It therefore carries with it, as a direct result of these attitudes, a mature, rich and integrated acceptance of the evils in the world.

The fact that there is *apartheid* in South Africa, for instance, is a fact that we are all supposed to be able to discuss objectively. It is also implicitly assumed that an objective discussion of the fact of *apartheid* in South Africa would not, of itself, arrive at the necessity of abolishing *apartheid* in South Africa. That would be a matter for the Prime Minister of South Africa and his government. The facts are objective: they concern existing interests in gold-mining, exports and imports, arms supplies and the right of traditional settlers to the land they settle. These are the facts as accepted by objectivity.

Any suggestion that these facts are only facts in the sense that they represent the state of affairs obtaining at the moment, any suggestion that these facts ought to be changed into non-facts, is treated as a lapse in objectivity. The same arguments are deployed by objectivity about Greece, Communist satellites, most South American states and so on. Concern for the existing facts is a business for missionaries, the Red Cross, or whomever it may be, perhaps the United Nations. Such facts as human suffering, perhaps even on a massive scale, are not facts for objectivity, whose prime concern is to evaluate the best means of preserving the *status quo*: the facts of human suffering are non-facts for objectivity, are merely subjective. It is always in the interests of objectivity to recognize (officially) those facts which best fit in with its own interests.

Secondly, objectivity, when defined as the political *status quo*, whether in Europe, Russia, Greece, South Africa or America, believes that it is not called upon to justify publicly the policies and acts it is responsible for. It refuses to call into question the moral criteria which govern its decisions. It refuses to shift or suspend, even momentarily, its perspectives on the world or to examine its policies from the pont of view of any of its critics, even critics of eminence within its own intellectual structure. Objectivity sets itself up as impersonal, as utterly devoted to the common good, and therefore refuses all subjective critique, in whatever form it may be offered – individual, racial, humanitarian, ethical. These are not the concern of objectivity. Objectivity insists upon the acceptance by the body politic of the facts offered to it as objectively valid. *All* criticism of this political objectivity is therefore, by definition, inimical to objectivity and can be pursued accordingly. Criticism of objectivity in our own societies is called 'radical', 'communist', 'subjective', and behind the Iron Curtain, 'revisionist', 'capitalist', etc. The terms may be different, but the reality is the same: objectivity does not like to be criticized.

Thirdly, objectivity selects what it intends to consider very carefully. It selects those parts of a problem which are either quantifiable or empirically governable or both. There is a continuous retreat from the general to the particular, from the whole to the parts, from the difficult to the simple, from the complex to the naïve, from the adequate to the banal. In all this, the belief in the quantifiability of data and the advent of the computer have helped objectivity enormously. They have made possible a simple refusal to discuss the human aspects of any subject whatsoever.

Objectivity has ended up as being the equivalent of that truncated fragment of rationality which is generally called scientific. In the scientific objectivity, the thinker is excluded from the thought, and the personal involvement of the thinker in his work is denied and frustrated. Subjectivity is excluded from the work in hand, all ethical criteria are divided sharply off from the pure scientific effort. In philosophy, for instance, human expressivity is no longer a creative function in the world, but the raw material for an infinitely complicated classification and analysis. Language has been put in chains so that philosophy can document and classify (and thereby render harmless) the extrusion of human subjectivity into the world.

Science as objectivity thus comes to be opposed to Romanticism in any form, to the presence of the individual in his work, to his subjectivity as ethical presence in the world, to the concept of the natural and the complete, to the demand for life as opposed to survival in a narrow biological sense. Objectivity has, in its very exclusiveness, defined itself as hostile to the values of the total man. Objectivity in the social sciences has thus become synonymous with the anti-subjective, the anti-human, the anti-life, in our culture. It is the split that F. R. Leavis refers to when he contrasts the 'technologico-Benthamism' of our society with values of 'Life' as presented by Blake, Dickens and Lawrence. It is the split Marcuse refers to in his concept of the 'one-dimensional man'. It is the split that the young Romantics indict when they select the university as a particularly striking example of intellectual disintegration.

And what are the major structures of our current scientific objectivity?

T. S. Kuhn, in his daring book *The Structure of Scientific Revolutions*,* has advanced the theory that behind all current work in the sciences, behind the rules, proceedings and assumptions of what he calls 'normal science' there hovers a 'paradigm'. This paradigm is largely undefinable, but it is a kind of conceptual ideal which informs and inspires all the thinking of a given society,

* University of Chicago Press, 2nd edn, 1970.

directs its interests and establishes for that society a strong sense of its own objectivity. 'Normal science', working with a kind of implicit faith in this paradigm, goes on 'puzzle-solving' at a low theoretical pressure until it reaches some problem it cannot solve under the aegis of its paradigm, there is a crisis of conceptuality, and this is when 'revolutionary science' is born.

Our own paradigm of objectivity in the sciences, a paradigm which we might call materialist-determinist-behaviourist-positivist, has a very interesting lineage behind it. It has been building up, into its present complex solidity, for three centuries at least. We can perhaps get an insight into its nature, as an operative set of ideal assumptions today, if we look up the *Encyclopedia Britannica* under the entry *'Behaviourism'* :

Many developments in the history of thought may be seen as precursors of Behaviourism, and some may be said to have led up to it in a fairly definite way. Among the former may be mentioned materialist and mechanist philosophy, especially in the modern period (e.g. Thomas Hobbes in the 17th century; the English empiricists and associationists of the 18th and 19th centuries; and such materialist philosophers of the French enlightenment as J. O. de Lamettrie and P. J. G. Cabanis); the dominance of the mechanical world view in the physical science of the 18th and 19th centuries and its penetration into biology; the positivism of the French sociologist-philosopher August Comte, who explicitly repudiated introspection as a basis for psychology as early as 1838.

The *Encyclopedia Britannica* further lists, as influences upon J. B. Watson, the founder of theoretical behaviourism, animal psychology, objectivistic biology, Russian reflexology and American philosophic pragmatism. 'Behaviourism', asserts the *Encyclopedia Britannica*, 'is first and foremost an extension of the methods of animal

psychology to the study of man.' And Watson himself, rejecting that brand of 'functionalism' which was an attempt
to replace Wundt-Titchener's 'chemistry' of consciousness,
wrote in 1913: 'The time seems to have come when psychology must discard all reference to consciousness; when
it need no longer delude itself into thinking that it is making mental states the object of observation.' Psychology
was to become 'a purely objective, experimental branch of
natural science'.

Does not all this hover as a paradigm, in Kuhn's sense,
behind contemporary objectivity in the universities and in
politics? Do we not immediately recognize it as the sort of
dominant *presupposition* in our societies? And is not its relationship to the reductive rationalism of the seventeenth
century also striking? There are so many family resem-
blances in the various historical visages of our paradigm.

One of the main characteristics of a paradigm is its in-
tolerance of criticism. A paradigm precedes, both logic-
ally and temporally, the actual thinking and research in a
society, being for these lower forms of intellection a kind
of controlling inspiration. It exists in a rarefied atmos-
phere, and its servants guard its reputation jealously.

Kuhn's book does of course, if only implicitly, throw
into question the dominant paradigm of objectivity in our
society. In the course of establishing the fact that science
moves in a kind of dialectic of advance and consolidation,
he has to suggest that science is not one unimpeded flow
of objective achievement. A paradigm is only in place
until a better one replaces it, and the obvious implication
is that our own objectivity, not eternal as we had taken it
to be, may one day be forced to suffer the ignominious
defeat of so many of its predecessors. Current objectivity
is not, that is to say, objectivity itself, it is just one temporary form of it.

It is interesting to see how violently his objective critics react to this suggestion. (Kuhn does not say it explicitly, but his critics are quick to sniff the implications.) In a collection of essays on Kuhn's work, published under the title *Criticism and the Growth of Knowledge** various philosophers of science, the self-appointed guardians of our objectivity, take Kuhn to task for his temerity.

One of the things which most offends Kuhn's objective critics is his comparison of normal science and its objective paradigm to theology, to a narrow and dogmatic orthodoxy to which novices are only admitted after intensive selection and training. To the guardians of objectivity, the very suggestion that normal science and its paradigm might be seen as a dogma is an outrage. For it is part of the very life-lie of our objectivity that it is totally open to reasoned, even radical (but not revolutionary!), criticism, at all levels, from all comers, at all times.

But if this were true, why are the objective philosophers of science after Kuhn in full-throated cry, like a pack of hounds after the fox? Kuhn's distinction between 'normal' and 'revolutionary' science is rejected in turn by Watkins (p. 37), by Toulmin (pp. 44-5), by Popper (p. 55), Lakatos (p. 178, where he asserts that *'in Kuhn's view scientific revolution is irrational, a matter for mob psychology'*) and by Feyerabend (pp. 208-9). There is a great deal of heat engendered in this supposedly objective discussion of Kuhn's theory of science. Only Margaret Masterman, with massive common-sense, asserts:

Far from querying the existence of Kuhn's 'normal science', I am going to assume it. . . . That there is normal science – and that it is exactly as Kuhn says it is – is the outstanding, the crashingly obvious fact which confronts and hits any philo-

* Edited by Imre Lakatos and Alan Musgrave, Cambridge University Press, 1970.

sophers of science who set out, in a practical or technological manner, to do any actual scientific research. It is because Kuhn – at last – has noticed this central fact about all real science ... that actual scientists are now, increasingly reading Kuhn instead of Popper: to such an extent, indeed, that, in new scientific fields particularly, 'paradigm' and not 'hypothesis' is now the 'O.K. word' [p. 6o].

We begin to see from this what is at issue: the Popperian orthodoxy has been challenged, and the paradigm of scientific objectivity which has reigned up to now is about to be deposed. A new priest now inhabits the sacred wood. Margaret Masterman, sensibly assuming that the new priest is conscious of the implications of his own achievement, writes: 'It is thus scientifically urgent, as well as philosophically important, to try to find out what a Kuhnian paradigm is' (p. 6o). She sets out to analyse the twenty-one different meanings that Kuhn's paradigm can have, and her speculation is thus a constructive reaction to Kuhn's suggestion, and not a mere irate rejection, a testy muttering about '*mob psychology*', in the manner of the objectivists.

Is there, in the social sciences, any current ongoing work which seems to embody the objective paradigm in a particularly pure form? Is there anywhere we can watch it in action, where it is supremely uncritical of itself as objectivity? It seems that the work of H. J. Eysenck is one of the most striking examples available. Eysenck works as close as he can to the paradigm of objectivity, and has obviously nothing but contempt for the concept of inner *experience* as such. And his work still obeys implicitly the early twentieth-century behaviourist paradigm of objectivity, the attempt that is to reduce all 'experience, no matter how complex, to a combination of ultimate elements' (*Encyclopedia Britannica*). Standing as close as he does to the original paradigm of Wundt-Titchener-Pavlov-Watson reductive objectivity, he is a particularly instructive example of the fact that our paradigm has not changed significantly since those early days.

In *The Structure of Human Personality** and *Personality Structure and Measurement*† statistical and quantifying analysis of human subjective experience is given its *reductio ad absurdum*. The objective paradigm of the natural sciences is clearly in evidence. Eysenck's model is mathematical and statistical.

But, over against the columns of decimalized figures (an impressive gesture towards the objective paradigm) one must however set the diagrams which scatter his pages, and which are medieval, not to say astrological, in conceptual primitiveness. They represent the unexamined side of the paradigm. Eysenck's leading idea of 'personality' as extraverted/introverted, neurotic/balanced, etc., has not in fact advanced beyond the stage of the poetic medieval metaphor of the 'four humours'‡ and the attempt to mathematize *that* is the modern equivalent of alchemy. The naïveté which leads him to believe that the answers given to his intimate questionnaires actually correspond to the *reality* about a person (instead of to what the person wants to believe, or even to the mere limits of his ability to conceptualize any verbal answer *at all* to a question about what is, for him, a lived subjective reality) is only matched by the sophistication of the statistical method of recording his 'results'. Rabbit, rat or human – all's one. There are the objective figures for all to see. 'Behaviourism is first and foremost an extension of the

---

* Methuen, 1953, 3rd edn, 1970.

† Routledge & Kegan Paul, 1969.

‡ Wundt's theory of the four temperaments is discussed at pp. 14ff. of *Personality Structure and Measurement*.

methods of animal psychology to the study of man' (*Encyclopedia Britannica*). In its unexamined objectivity, the experimental work of 1969 still obeys the theoretical behests of 1913.

H. J. Eysenck is interesting, not in himself (for behaviourism will pass away as an inadequate paradigm when the subjective crisis of our world makes itself fully present to consciousness) but as a *typical* example of a research worker who serves the Kuhnian paradigm of 'normal', 'puzzle-solving' science as faithfully as he can. This 'puzzle-solving' activity can only proceed while the paradigm is in place, and this activity does not attempt any major conceptual modifications in the paradigm, being content to do piece-work within its protection.

Eysenck's work is thus typical, unexamined objectivity in action, still operating with those early twentieth-century ideas of behavioural theory, pragmatism and positivism which were bright ideas in their time. Eysenck's work shows us that the paradigm hasn't changed. No doubt Eysenck will continue, as will the majority of his co-workers, to collect statistics until the old 'puzzle-solving', 'normal' science of our century is clearly seen to have reached the limits of its credibility. At that point, some kind of Kuhnian 'revolutionary science' will be a life-necessity.

Meanwhile, objectivity such as Eysenck's experimental alchemy is such a typical example of, fits in harmoniously with, a cooling political climate. Objectivity, both eastern and western, sees advantages in the political use of behavioural expertise. It is increasingly obvious that the *control* of behaviour, which started off as an interesting experimental idea, has now passed out of the laboratory and become a political capital of the first importance.

It is not, of course, the work of Eysenck unaided, but

of the whole philosophical-psychological-experimental naïveté of our objective paradigm which has let this happen. The whole flow of unexamined objectivity in the first half of this century has brought it about. And the results are beginning to appear.

The knowledge we can gain of human beings under laboratory conditions can help us 'control' large masses of people in the future. This knowledge is always of weaknesses (determinisms) and never of strengths (freedoms to react spontaneously). We can protect ourselves from human nature by controlling it (setting the mechanisms) in advance. (Eysenck, for example, even believes that we can identify our future criminals in advance and treat them accordingly in time: this view has been taken seriously at high administrative levels in the United States.) The human being is a machine like any other machine in a universe governed exclusively by mechanical and physiological laws. As in the physical sciences, so in the psychological sciences, the methods of quantitative measurement, controlled experiment and programmed prediction are suitable (fitting). The mechanisms of the brain and body are, as physiological constructs, more or less totally determined in advance. Surprises (freedoms), if there are any, will doubtless be eliminated in some later reduction. If they cannot, they can be ignored as random elements in an otherwise totally determined system of physical-chemical-nervous causality. We can contrive, by experiment, to control the total human phenomenon, down to its smallest parts in their inter-related dependence, and thus 'understand' the whole at the micro-action level. It is assumed that the whole is not greater than the sum of the parts, and that a complete explanation of the workings of the parts will exhaust *all* the active possibilities of the physiological machine under discussion. The behavioural scientist can now 'prevent us in all our doings', as the Prayer Book has it. Man cannot transcend this network of objectivity at any point. Man is no more.

It is obvious to Konrad Lorenz, for example, that the American political objectivity in particular more or less coincides with a behaviourist model of objectivity. Political objectivity has reduced man to parts just as the psychologists of the inclined plane have. He expresses this idea trenchantly in a recent interview in *L'Express* (June 1970):

This simplified doctrine of the conditioned reflex does everything it can to annihilate its enemies. One has to be a bit of a Don Quixote to fight against it. This doctrine, which I call 'pseudo-democratic', has deep roots and is even dangerous. For the theory according to which man is only the creation of his environment is comfortable for everyone – the citizen who has been 'equalized' in this way is welcome both to American capitalism which hopes for obedient consumers and to the leader of a totalitarian system which hopes for a citizen without surprises.... If ... one observes the mental and emotional resistance which the behaviourists have for everything that is not conditioned reflex, one finds, I think, in the background, the ideology of all the current political doctrines ... Any man who wishes to 'manage' the big masses automatically adheres to the equalizing doctrine of the all-powerful conditioned reflex.

The conditioning of the reflexes of the political animals in America is thus linked explicitly by Lorenz with the behaviourist assumptions of American psychology. Behaviourism as objectivity creates a climate of opinion where the objective view of the world fits in closely with the lie of the political facts, the facts that have to be recognized if society is going to get the protection (say, from the Communists) that it needs. Any objection raised to this objectivity belongs, as Lorenz says, to the order of the merely quixotic.

Behaviourist psychology shares at least this with positivist philosophy, that it has reduced the study of meaning to the study of language, it has reduced the whole intentional message to the elements of the code. This reduction has in fact metaphysical as well as political implications. For the original signifying message is not accepted as an enterprise of freely operating intentionality, but is studied purely as a categorizable set of units which can be broken down into as nearly as possible invariant rules.

Behaviourist and positivist science thus regard the human animal not so much as a signifying totality in the world, calling for intelligent reaction from his counter-subjects in the world, but as a largely unconscious emitting centre with the same signifying value as a buoy with a bell on, moved passively from beneath by the swell of his environment. The message emitted is taken to be largely involuntary, unconscious, law-governed, necessitated. Lorenz is not the only critic of the behaviourist attitude to have pointed out the underlying desire to deny and restrict human freedom inherent in that attitude. The signifying creativity, which Chomsky has in a famous review* of Skinner's *Verbal Behaviour* established as a basic freedom in human beings, is treated by the behaviourists with suspicion and dislike. For behaviourism it is the message which is of interest, not the emitting subject in the world. It is not his *meaning* in terms of his own projects which catches their attention, but his *language* in so far as it can be fitted into pre-existing behavioural models.

For the same reason, it is difficult not to recognize in proxemics (the work of Edward Hall) and in kinesics (the

* Reprinted in Fodor and Katz, *The Structure of Language*, 1964.

work of R. Birdwhistell) two new forms of reductionist behaviourism. Hall, for instance, reduces our experience of space to four distances, Intimate, Personal, Social, Public. He even assigns feet and inches to these distances. Each of us is supposed to feel the categorized distance come into operation at exactly the same place. Intimate distance can range from physical contact in its 'Close Phase' up to 18 inches in its 'Far Phase'. Personal Distance in its 'Close Phase' is 1½–2½ feet and in its 'Far Phase' 2½–4 feet. Social Distance, Hall assures us, comes into being in its 'Close Phase' at 4–7 feet and in its 'Far Phase' from 7–12 feet. Public Distance, finally, is fixed in its 'Close Phase' between 12–15 feet (Hall suggests this may be a vestigial form of animal 'flight' distance) and in its 'Far Phase' at 25 feet or more.*

But it is significant that these fixed distances have been worked out for human beings on a model suggested by H. Hediger's work on the territoriality of animals in his Zürich zoo. It is a noticeable feature of *The Hidden Dimension* that no significant distinction is made, either in terms of concepts or of level, either in terms of method or of approach, between the studies of contact species and non-contact species of *animals* in the first three chapters of the book, and the studies of *human* spatial experience developed in subsequent chapters.

We recall the comment in the *Encyclopedia Britannica* article on Behaviourism: 'Behaviourism is first and foremost an extension of the methods of animal psychology to the study of man', and in the light of this comment, we seem to have ample grounds for asking ourselves whether, in spite of its newfangled name, *proxemics* is any advance on early twentieth-century behavioural method.

* Edward Hall, *The Hidden Dimension*, Doubleday, New York, 1966 (The Bodley Head, 1969), chapter 10.

Hall is another interestingly typical example of the persistence of the objective paradigm through various sciences, old and new, and across half a century. Hall seems to be totally unconscious of making an immediate unanalysed transition from one sort of documentation (overcrowding of rats) to another (spatial codes of human beings). This objective, quantifying, behavioural transition is so natural to Hall that he is not even aware that he is making it, and therefore, makes no effort to protect himself against charges of methodological naïveté. He simply acts in accordance with his inherited paradigm of objectivity. As Margaret Masterman says so acutely in *Criticism and the Growth of Knowledge*: 'The paradigm is something which can function when the theory is not there' (p. 66).

Hall admits, in *The Silent Language** as well as in *The Hidden Dimension*, that spatial and temporal habits vary *cross-culturally*, that space and time are accorded different values in different cultures. But he never thinks of human space as something *sui generis*, which belongs to the inner intentional world of each individual. For him, German space is given the value 'x', Arab space the value 'y' and so on. All Germans and Arabs are supposed to conform automatically to this arbitrary grid.

The question as to whether differences of spatial tolerance might not come into operation at variable points in each individual case, and the question as to whether, therefore, cross-cultural comparisons are quantifiable at all, just never arise. Neither does the interesting possibility (fundamental to the theory of indirect communication) that the individual might use space *contrapuntally*, in such a way as to *counter* received cultural expectations. The question doesn't arise in *proxemics* because, objectively, there is

* Doubleday, New York, 1959.

no conceptual difference between the signalling resources of animals and men.

The work of Ray Birdwhistell testifies to the same deeply-lying behavioural assumptions. Birdwhistell has set himself the unenviably difficult task of analysing human non-verbal communication (paralinguistics) in terms of its minimal gestures and combinations thereof. This study he calls *kinesics*. The smallest perceptible units of bodily expressivity he calls *kines*, and these are painstakingly recorded in little ideograms of face, head, hands, body and so on, as these are used to signify.* But 'no *kine* ever stands alone' (p. 15). *Kines* are strung together in significantly recurring sets, called *kinemorphs*, and it is in their significant variation within the *kinemorphs* that *kines* set up differential meaning (p. 16).

So far so good. But Birdwhistell, like Hall, wants to do analysis in terms of signs which have been established (experimentally) as *univocal*. Birdwhistell writes of 'the necessity of deriving an orthography by means of which the particles of motion can be isolated and their pattern activity and significance empirically tested. Particularly is this necessary if we are to do cross-cultural analysis' (p. 14).

This is not so good. It is a type of thinking which conforms uncritically to the behaviourist-experimental objective paradigm. Indeed, Birdwhistell is quite open about this:

I believe that by this method we are orienting the study of body motion in a direction whereby it will ultimately be possible to analyse *contextual meaning* empirically, and through scientific experimentation, rather than through the

* *Introduction to Kinesics* (*An annotation system for analysis of body motion and gesture*), University of Louisville, Kentucky, 1952.

often misleading devices concerning meaning derivation supplied by intuitionist philosophical approaches [p. 17].

Not so different from Watson's remark of 1913! The objective paradigm is still firmly in place, and still unquestioned.

And what is the inevitable result? It is that objectivity fails, as usual, to be adequately objective because it refuses to take subjective and unquantifiable data up into its synthesis. Birdwhistell's method of research emerges as yet another variety of formalism, yet another form of objective abstraction, which only intermittently overlaps the truth and variety of gestural significance, and this for a very good linguistic reason.

There is, that is to say, in Birdwhistell's approach a consistently carried through reduction of the particular gesture to the general rule or grammar derived deductively from previous experimentation. A certain gestural *langue* has been set up (as valid for this precise cultural group), and the laws of this *langue* worked out. Subsequent instances of already catalogued gestures will therefore be taken as having the same meaning-content as the ones that went before. Thus the individual *parole* is squashed back, so to speak, into the *langue* that has already been built up, and is effectively denied its own chance to signify in its own way. Instead of a new *parole* being allowed that signifying creativity that Chomsky postulates, instead of the new *parole* being allowed to set up a new signifying nexus in its own creative terms, and being allowed to stand as the first member of a new *langue* which it is itself trying to constitute and to bring into being, it is forced back into the matrix of previous experimental data.

Birdwhistell thus consistently and deliberately emasculates every new sign, referring it backwards to what he

has worked out already. After a certain point he will therefore cease to learn anything new at all, and his visual sense
will operate *a priori*.

Birdwhistell's research would be unexceptionable if
each gesture were interpreted as the subjective response of
a *given* human subjectivity to *given* experienced conditions, and thus described as a unique case in some larger
hermeneutic exercise. In his recent book *Kinesics and Context** for instance, Birdwhistell analyses at great length
'Doris's' remark : 'I suppose all mothers think their kids are
smart, but I have no worries about that child's intellectual
ability' (p. 228). Birdwhistell writes : 'In this exercise our
focus is upon what Doris *says* in this situation. It is not our
present problem to determine what she *means*' (p. 235).
That is just as well, because, until we know who 'Doris' *is*,
we have not the slightest chance of discovering what she
means. Of her actual spoken-cum-gestural utterance we
can, of course, go on speculating and drawing up kinesic-
linguistic transcriptions till the cows come home.

The connection between the gesture and the code is not,
as Birdwhistell assumes, direct or objectively fixable. It remains resolutely subjective and individual. The connection between gesture and code, between *parole* and
langue, has to be established anew for every individual, in
every situation, on every occasion. But Birdwhistell re-
jects this suggestion with *hauteur*. This means 'he abdi-
cates his professional role and interprets as an amateur, as
do other members of society'† – and what could be worse

* Allen Lane The Penguin Press, 1971.
† ibid., p. 82. See also pp. 80-81 : 'We have been unable to discover any single facial expression, stance, or body position which
conveys an identical meaning in all societies.' Does Birdwhistell
really believe that there is any single facial expression, etc., which
would convey an identical meaning in *any* society?

than that? The principle of treating each sign as an intentional unity is of course anathema to objectivity, bringing as it does all intra- and cross-cultural rule-building activities to a halt.*

The objective, given, observable *gesture*, the signal, the facial expression, is taken as being *sufficient* for purposes of analysis by Birdwhistell, as it is by Michael Argyle in England. 'Gestures are movements of hands, feet or other parts of the body,' Argyle assures us in *The Psychology of Interpersonal Behaviour*.† The proposition alone might give us reason to pause. Is that *all* a gesture is? What would it be signifying, for instance? 'Facial expression can be reduced to changes in eyes, brows, mouth and so on' (ibid., pp. 35-6). Can it though? 'Emotions can be recognized to some extent from facial expression alone, as is shown by studies using still photographs of actors' (p. 36). This rather gives the game away : the double abstraction, first from life and then from realism, does not seem to worry Argyle at the level of evidence. A curiously primitive diagram follows (p. 36) which is worth studying for an insight into what is acceptable as evidence, as a starting point, by objectivity (and Michael Argyle is eminently objective). 'In addition to these states, it is possible to recognize degrees of emotional tension – by perspiration on the forehead and expansion of the pupils of the eyes,' ends Argyle triumphantly, with the air of having told us something. If the gesture, the sweating and distended pupils are irrefragable evidence of the existence of the corresponding emotion in the subject, then it is surprising that any actor portraying Hamlet lasts more than a night or two.

* Julius Fast's *Body Language* (Souvenir Press, London, 1970) is the *reductio ad absurdum* of Birdwhistell's method.

† Penguin Books, 1967, p. 33.

Emotion and sign need not necessarily coincide. Signs can be used contrapuntally, or even deliberately to deceive. There is no automatic transformation in either direction.

The later analyses of Argyle are vitiated, as are Birdwhistell's, by this initial, unquestioned assumption, that *a* gesture has *a* meaning, that certain groups of 'typical' gestures may be taken as quantitatively invariable under certain social conditions. If the presuppositions of the investigation are unquestioned in this naïve but objective way, it is not surprising that behaviourist psychology never tells us anything that we could not have observed for ourselves on the bus.

For gestures are not only, of course, 'movements of hands, feet or other parts of the body', as Argyle so easily assumes. They are a complex exteriorization of a vast range of inner choices and decisions in the gesturing subject. He has to exteriorize his feelings as best he may, and many forms of doing that may seem good to him at different times and in different conditions. His control over his gestures may be greater or less. His aim to impress, excuse, condole, reassure, will modify the choice he makes of his gesture. The gesture *itself*, the signal *itself* is not *sufficient* for the purposes of analysis. One has to get behind the gesture to the originating subjectivity for whom that gesture has a meaning, a specific meaning. *The meaning transcends the sign in which it is enclosed.* To this proposition, of course, objectivity can give no assent.

The gesture is not sufficient evidence because it depends upon a context, and an intention, both of which are 'within' the subject. Objectivity will not, cannot, take account of incommensurables like these (subjective context, intention), even when they amount to more than half of the evidence. They are rejected because not *quanti-*

fiable. Because not quantifiable, it is claimed that they are not *relevant*. But the conclusion does not follow from the premise.

Objectively, it is the sign which is given, the gesture, and for objectivity that is all there is, that is enough. But the subjective strata of the message, sign or gesture all lie behind the outward form of the message, as the Post Office lies behind the telegram. Behind the signs, behind the words we emit, is the vast hinterland of subjective intention, that 'primordial silence' as Merleau-Ponty called it, which precedes and makes possible all language, and with it, ability to choose just this message or gesture rather than that one.

Reversing the thought-progress of behaviouristic objectivity then, we could say that behind the gesture lies the context and the intention. Behind them lies the subjective hinterland of unknown causes. And behind that lies the 'primordial silence' which makes expression possible at all.

Two movements in this century have significantly challenged the premises of objectivity in psychology and philosophy: they are phenomenology and Gestalt theory. Both have more or less failed, partly because of the intrinsic difficulties of what they were trying to achieve, and partly because the objective tide was flowing the other way. Both phenomenology and Gestalt, dealing as they do in the idea of the *totality* of phenomena instead of the parts thereof, were necessarily in for a choppy passage.

If we look back to an early paper in the history of Gestalt theory, a paper of Max Wertheimer's dating from 1925, we get a double vision. There are the immense, the exciting, the adult, the adequate implications of what Wertheimer says and suggests, and, just a second after, we glimpse the unlikelihood of such an intelligent, such an

unquantifiable approach as that of Gestalt getting anywhere in the booming scientific population explosion of
our century. Wertheimer writes:

It has long seemed obvious – and is, in fact, the characteristic tone of European science – that 'science' means breaking
up complexes into their component elements. Isolate the elements, discover all their laws, then reassemble them, and the
problem is solved. All wholes are reduced to pieces and piece-
wise relations between pieces.

The fundamental 'formula' of Gestalt theory might be expressed in this way: There are wholes, the behaviour of which
is not determined by that of their individual elements, but
where the part-processes are themselves determined by the
intrinsic nature of the whole. It is the hope of Gestalt theory
to determine the nature of such wholes.

With a formula such as this one might close, for Gestalt
theory is neither more nor less than this.*

In fact, as a second paper of Wertheimer's clearly
shows, the idea of taking the *totality* of the phenomena
seriously was really central to Gestalt theory:

The given is itself in varying degrees 'structured' (*gestaltet*),
it consists of more or less definitely structured wholes and
whole-processes with their whole-properties and laws, characteristic whole-tendencies and whole-determinations of parts.
'Pieces' almost always appear 'as parts' in whole processes.†

'Whole-determinations of parts'! Objectivity has no
conceptual apparatus for understanding that, for the direction is 180 degrees away from quantifiability. And so it
was too with phenomenology, the basic effort of which is

---

* 'Gestalt theory' by Max Wertheimer, in *A Source Book of
Gestalt Psychology*, ed. W. D. Ellis, Kegan Paul, 1938.
† ibid., p. 14. The paper dates from 1922.

to understand the totality of the subjective from *the inside*, using only the analytic devices of description, hermeneutics and gloss. Those are primitive instruments, but at least they need not distort the materials under review. But, like Gestalt theory, phenomenology was trying to get something said about what really *matters*, the essential, and so it was, in a world increasingly objective, bound to be overwhelmed sooner or later.

Nevertheless, in spite of the fact that both paths peter out in the depths of the forest, their direction was certainly correct, and the urgent task is to constitute a method which would carry on from where they left off. In psychology itself there have been some quite striking successes already in the work of R. D. Laing and his team. *Families of Schizophrenics** tells us about space, not as measured in feet and inches, but as experienced by a suffering schizophrenic in a tiny home occupied by constricting and repressive parents or relations. Laing describes experienced space, not measured space. This is achieved through the study of the *totality* and by working *from the inside*. It is a success because it is not objective in the normal impoverished sense, but takes objectivity *seriously enough* to examine subjectivity subjectively.

Laing consistently urges the case for the transcendence of signification over the brute givenness of the message, gesture or sign. His quotation from Kraepelin at page 29 of *The Divided Self†* sends a frisson down the spine. How could any analyst have been so brutal, so literal, so unseeing as Kraepelin? 'When asked where he is, he says, "You want to know that too? I tell you who is being measured and is measured and shall be measured. I know all that, and

---

* By R. D. Laing and A. Esterson, vol. 1 of *Sanity, Madness and the Family*, Tavistock Press, 1964.

† Penguin Books, 1965.

could tell you, but I do not want to." ' But Kraepelin's attitude is *still* the dominant one. Behaviourism measures away, unaware that it is itself measured. The 'signs' it interprets from its schizophrenics and catatonics it takes absolutely seriously, at face value, all the 'gestures' of 'hands, feet or other parts of the body' are measured, recorded, stored in computers. And what the patient is *saying* never gets heard. Kraepelin's catatonic patient is still being measured in units which have no further existence or reality than their occupancy of a tape or card. And he is still measuring.

Behaviourism, objectivity, just cannot *explain* enough about human expressivity in the world. There is too much left over, too vast a hinterland of unexplained and irreducible subjectivity for the explanations of behaviourism to satisfy us. Who can explain the film and the event of *Woodstock*, for instance? Behaviourism certainly cannot, because it cannot classify the units (in the manner of Birdwhistell) which went to make up this vast mosaic of subjective messages. The meaning transcends the component parts of the emitted messages. In *Woodstock* the human body is *used*, it is used to *signify*, it becomes a plastic medium in which a powerful message is moulded out of modern clay. But the message is thrown away as soon as sent, a useless toy. Behind the message remains the welling source of all meaning, free, unconstrained, unquantifiable.

At the root of both political and social-scientific failures in adequate objectivity is the radical failure of philosophy to understand the age in which it is living. No ideological advances can be made if there is not an adequate philosophical foundation, and that foundation has been notably lacking in British and American philosophy since at least the last World War, probably earlier.

British and American philosophy may be described as positivist: not in a narrowly defined sense, but in a large sense which includes all the varieties of philosophical activity at present dominating the intellectual field. To say that philosophy is positivist implies that it is ideologically incapable of taking account of the root problems of the world we live in. Philosophy and the world should fit each other like hand and glove. There has been no fit for several decades now.

To some extent, the absorption of philosophy in language-games has created the climate in which the present effusion of linguistic sciences could come about. The philosophical climate and the linguistic effusion together add up to an interest in language which excludes an interest in meaning: a strange paradox, and one only visible from that distance away from both at which the wood is quite distinct from the trees.

If philosophy has narrowed its interests as much as it has, to the discussion of problems of meaning expounded and protected by a tiny number of philosophers who maintain a jealous monopoly of all philosophical discourse, then it follows naturally enough that philosophy cannot be in any living contact with the problems of meaning as they are experienced by the great masses of people in the world. Its very exclusiveness guarantees its provinciality. That provinciality is at the moment a matter of pride to the monopoly: but constitutes in fact a total failure of objectivity.

It is a mark of objectivity that it prefers the model to the living whole, the paradigm to the reality, the parts to the totality. A kind of Uriah Heep-like modesty has long been in vogue, a modesty which would not attempt to do more than regulate the pronouncements of scientists in their own fields, examining and commenting upon the conditions under which what has already been done in science has in fact been done. This modesty is the modesty of the cuckoo who places her eggs in another nest. Science is not interested in the regulative activities of the philosophers, and the philosophers do not interest the world in general.

They could hardly do so when their concept of meaning is so impoverished. Meaning is, of course, wider than verbal. Meaning is just as easily living meaning, the meaning of intersubjective space, art, the lived body, signs of all kinds, the activities of war and peace. None of these comes under the purview of philosophy as at present constituted. Those who would look for philosophical guidance to the meaning of the modern world as a totality have to go elsewhere. There is, of course, one very obvious place to go: into the large theoretical arms of all-explaining Marxism. The present wave of enthusiasm for that philosophy among the young Romantics is a direct result of the Western philosophical failure. When they do embrace Marxism, it is *faute de mieux*, since there have been no ideological barricades for them to shelter behind in a world in which ideology has already very largely replaced philosophy in the old sense.

Indeed, philosophy is so far from being adequately objective at the moment that it is actually contemptuous of ideology. Positivism has steered resolutely clear of existential, ideological and political problems. Positivism and empiricism have nothing but contempt, it would seem, for the anguish of a world where the continued existence of philosophy is itself problematic, and, in many countries already, illegal. Such contempt is insolent.

Apart from being insolent, it represents a failure of objectivity in an adequate sense, in that too much has been left out of consideration. The preference for the parts to the whole can end up as a game of chess in which each side is allowed to play with only two pieces. Of course, a check-mate is ultimately possible, but only in the absence of that network of signifying units which would have made the game a complete and real one.

How much can philosophy in fact afford to leave out of consideration and still claim to be objective? Scorn is poured on the woolly idealists beyond the Channel and the 'incredible vapourings' of ideologists like Marx and Guevara, and contempt is taken as a sufficient attitude before the menace of ideology. Philosophy seems to believe that as long as it keeps on talking about verification, propositions, strict logical entailment, induction, private languages, other minds and so on, its activities can be taken as rational.

But, in fact, in the face of the present demand for rationality (adequate objectivity) this pseudo-objectivity represents the most absolute apostasy from rationality. The philosophers dress up to play their favourite game, 'objectivity'. It is an embarrassing re-occurrence of the problem of the Emperor's clothes. An admirable desire for accuracy and method turns into charade. The complacent view that objectivity is alive and well and living in Oxford is, in our day, unacceptable.

Philosophy refuses (like all objectivity) to open up the discussion at the level of its own *raison d'être*. It refuses to offer its own justification for its existence in the world. Naturally, philosophy spends most of its time discussing: criteria precisely! But not the criteria by which its own existence is justified in the modern world. Philosophy spends most of its time discussing the conditions under which something might or might not be meaningful, verifiable, and so on, but never gets to the fundamental problem of discussing the meaning of philosophy itself. This woeful foreshortening of perspective has fatal results for philosophy. Its objectivity is reduced to that of the philosophers and scientists whom Gulliver encounters in the Grand Academy of Lagado during his Voyage to Laputa.

Not only does philosophy refuse to take account of the major ideologists of our world and attempt a reasoned reply to them, but it protects its own inviolable sanctity with a single-mindedness that can only be described as morbid. Philosophy is, of course, desperately concerned to defend its own objectivity, the objectivity of the academy and the Schools. There, the slightest hint, the merest whiff, of unorthodoxy is enough for a gasp of shock, questioning glances, nervous smiles. It is assumed that there are certain things which philosophy is able to do, certain things which philosophy is prepared to talk about, certain philosophers whose word is unquestioned and others whose name may not even be mentioned. *Procul, o procul este, profani!* The temple of divine philosophy shall not be soiled by the presence of unbelievers and heretics. To 'do philosophy' in our universities today demands the most unquestioning submission to orthodoxy and transmitted authority, to the popes and bishops and the laying on of hands which ensures a pure continuation of uncontaminated gnosis. When established positivism *has* to take account of a major ideologist of our time, the writer of the critique will confine himself to an exposé of the 'logical' mistakes made in the argument of a man whose work has modified the consciousness of millions. Thus the ideologist is rapped over the knuckles with the schoolmasterly ruler, while the ideology lies potent and active in the minds of a whole generation, untouched by any criticism at a sufficiently objective (ideological) level.

Philosophical orthodoxy refuses to deal with the objective problems raised by subjectivity in the world. The Hippy philosophy of passivity, dropping-out and unconcern has its theoretical counterpart in the work of Heidegger for instance (the philosophy of *Gelassenheit* and shepherding of Being), but neither the lived passivity nor the philosophical statement interests philosophical objectivity. Che Guevara's subjective philosophy of harassment of the *status quo* by guerrilla tactics is a *praxis* which has had some success in the modern world, but it is no more interesting to philosophy than the theoretical writings of Régis Debray or even of Mao. Acute subjective dissatisfaction in the world is not mediated, analysed and confronted seriously by philosophy, on an adequate ideological level: it is just simply ignored. Therefore world Communism does not exist as a problem for objectivity, and its founders, themselves the subject of passionate dispute in most of Europe and much of America, not to mention the Communist world, are relegated in a folder to that dusty archive known by contemporary positivism as the History of Ideas.

It is significant in this respect that philosophical objectivity is conceptually (because visually) incapable of taking account of the cluster of phenomena and concepts which hover round the word 'revolution'. Numerous indeed are the assurances and reassurances that 'nothing like what is happening in America could happen here', or 'a revolution in this country is impossible (unthinkable)'.

These propositions are fair enough if they envisage revolution on the 1789 or the 1917 model, which they do. But the new types of internal revolution, carried on within a society, and which amount to a war of attrition, are not apparent to objectivity because it is untrained to recognize their forms. Objectivity cannot recognize the quiet *transformation of consciousness** through which we are passing in England and Europe at the moment, because it has not read the theoreticians of that quiet internal revolution. It calls them 'unreadable', and therefore does not read them. Objectivity is thus totally unequipped to deal with the very real menaces hidden within these new types of revolution, one of the most striking features of which is the desire to bring down the universities in chaos and to destroy the current intellectual norms of what is called a 'capitalist' or 'bourgeois' society.

The fact that objectivity refuses to read the theoreticians of the new revolution means that it renders itself progressively more incapable of dealing with the conceptual dangers hidden in them. Once again, the results of leaving the subjective factors out of analysis means an impoverished objectivity, an inadequate objectivity. Until the completely, radically, new concept of what a revolution is has filtered through to positivism, positivism will do only disservice to those who are trying to think rationally in our society. Positivism in fact weakens the cause of objectivity by refusing to consider the hidden structures of subjectivity.

What has philosophical objectivity left out of the analysis? Just subjectivity, nothing more or less. What kind of objectivity is it, though, that can leave out of account all the political, existential and ethical problems of our time? If one collected together the names of those most despised

* Edgar Morin, in his *Journal de Californie* (Seuil, Paris, 1970) writes: 'I feel more strongly than ever that the word survival is becoming synonymous with the word revolution, that the word revolution is becoming synonymous with the word mutation. We are approaching the threshold where the questions of survival, of mutation and of revolution are going to become one and the same question' (p. 109). Morin *looks* at California, and he *cares* enough to take its subjectivity seriously.

by philosophical positivist objectivity for their contributions to contemporary thought, one would have a list of the men whose names will eventually stand for modern philosophy itself.

Philosophy's almost exclusive concern with language in our century has made the intensive study of linguistics into a quasi-philosophical pursuit, having large theoretical pretensions. Instead however of searching for human meaning and examining its importance for subjective existence in the world, linguistics has added its considerable prestige to the cause of that progressive formalization which, in psychology, sociology and philosophy, has already abstracted human meaning virtually out of concrete existence. In the same way that primitive psychology tries to fix invariant patterns and laws of human languages and behaviour, so linguistics, as a rapidly expanding sub-section of the prevailing objectivity in its own right, has weighed in on the side of ever-increasing formalization which already threatens human subjectivity at so many points.

In fact, what linguistics has done is to substitute the study of language for the study of meaning. The death of God proclaimed by several philosophers of the last century and of this has found a temporary remedy: language. Language has stepped in very helpfully to fill that vacuum which Nature is said to abhor, and has in fact stopped a considerable quantity of spiritual energy from streaming off into the void.

But the study of language can only be a transitory state, a moment of passage, when signification is artificially conferred upon some value so as to satisfy that deepest craving for meaning which the human mind cannot apparently smother for long. Language, as a useful stop-gap, a convenient half-way house between one state and another, serves no doubt a very useful purpose.

But the formalization (the intricacy, the difficulty, the magic of the undertaking) is in fact an attempt to fob off a demand for meaning with an offer of Science. A gap is opening up between meaning and the study of meaning, between language and the study of language. The subjective demand for meaning has begun to oppose itself to formalization, and the more philosophy and linguistics move off into their private realms of speculation, the more emphatic will be their rejection by subjective need in the world. What is becoming more and more urgent a necessity is in fact not subtle descriptions of meaning or language, but meaning and language themselves.

4

SUBJECTIVE
OBJECTIONS
TO
'OBJECTIVITY'

Are we, perhaps, *here* just for saying: House
Bridge, Fountain, Gate, Jug, Fruit tree, Window, –
possibly: Pillar, Tower? ... but for *saying*, remember,
oh, for such saying as never the things themselves
hoped so intensely to be.*

What would full and adequate objectivity be like? What
would it be like to re-encounter the world as a totality
in the manner Rilke so painfully reconstructs? What
methods, what trains of thought are open to us if we wish
to propose an alternative model of rationality, one which
takes into account the full reality and demands an answer
which satisfies our human need for an intelligible world?
Are we already totally helpless before the political-
scientific-objective impersonality of the latter half of
our twentieth century? Is it just unthinkable that we
should ever again be able to connect the effect with the
cause, the significance with the practice, the justification
with the practical ability?

It would appear that the only way to achieve this is to
cut the Gordian knot – by a swingeing ethical subjectivity
to call objectivity to the bar of human responsibility and
force it to offer its defence. Subjectivity deployed as ethical critique suddenly takes on a high *conceptual* value.

* R. M. Rilke, 'Ninth Elegy', *Duino Elegies*, translated by J. B.
Leishman and Stephen Spender, Hogarth Press, 1952, p. 85.

The student movement has indicated objectivity through action, being largely unable to formulate the concepts. Subjective objection to objectivity would be able to indict objectivity through the concept, thus transcending the need for simply obstructive action.

Even from within the sciences and philosophy there have come messages indicating that a struggle has been going on. Some of the blueprints drawn up for an adequate rationality have been explicitly philosophical. Some of these blueprints are impressive, while bearing the marks of imperfection and stress. No subjective philosophy which has had to fight for its existence *within* the autocratic world of objectivity ever springs fully armed like Minerva from the head of Jupiter. On the contrary, subjective philosophy has to struggle for its very existence against the *status quo* of reigning objectivity and offer what help it can in the face of fanatical opposition.

One remarkable attempt to draw up the guiding lines of an adequate objectivity has come from Edmund Husserl, the founder of phenomenology.* Very late in his life,

* Edmund Husserl (1859–1938), German mathematician, logician and philosopher, the founding father of phenomenology, is generally acknowledged to be one of the most influential figures in twentieth-century philosophy. He began as a mathematician, and came into conflict with Frege. Some of Frege's criticisms of his own work made him believe that relativity in all its forms was misleading, so he effected, in his *Logical Investigations* (1900–1901) a strenuous retreat from empiricism, positivism, nominalism and psychologism. He was fascinated by the problem of *meaning*, the study of which he made into his life's work. Logic deals with meaning, but so far it had undertaken the job very inadequately, especially in its objectivist refusal to deal with the subjective component of knowing, the way we actually *confer* a meaning upon the world. The relativists were wrong, but all previous philosophical approaches to meaning had been impoverishing and superficial. Husserl therefore saw the necessity of making an

when he was over seventy, he recorded his deep distress at the prevalence of false objectivity, or objectivism as he called it, and drew up a blueprint of a more adequate method of thinking.

Husserl felt that something had gone terribly wrong with European thinking right across the board. Towards the end of his life, this feeling became so acute that he referred to it as 'the crisis of European sciences'. Its main interest to us is perhaps not its obscure scheme of transcendental phenomenology (which seems to Husserl to be the way out) but its penetrating analysis of the historical evolution of the European split mind, the description of the

---

analysis of his own more radical than any historical one. The new inquiry should be pure, free from presuppositions of any kind, and would study the essence of experience in a rigorously scientific manner.

In order to study the phenomena of the mind (the only things we have certain knowledge of) he developed his own idea of phenomenology, which would be a study of 'the things themselves', that is to say the things of the mind as given unquestionably in mental experience. In 1907 he gave the lectures later published as *The Idea of Phenomenology* and in 1913, in his newly founded journal for phenomenological studies, he published the first part of his *Ideas for a Pure Phenomenology and Phenomenological Philosophy*. In this long essay he sketched out the main features of a method that he spent the rest of his life ceaselessly trying to make more explicit and to improve. He tried several times to introduce his system to the general public without much success. The *Paris Lectures* (1929), later transformed into *Cartesian Meditations* (1931) were such attempts. *The Crisis of European Sciences*, written in the last years of his life (1934-8), is his final effort. He wrote that 'for years he had been under the illusion that it would be a comparatively simple matter to write a "popular" introduction, but that in reality all his attempts throughout the last ten years, attempts which had resulted in the London and Paris lectures and the French *Méditations*, had been without satisfactory

historical events which led to the menacing dominance of objectivism in contemporary thought.

European philosophy has a *telos*, asserts Husserl, a kind of inner direction. This direction was set by the Greeks. It was the direction inspired by a belief in the dignity of man and his ability to understand the world he lives in and control it. Philosophy and science for the Greeks were there to help man in his daily life in what Husserl calls the *Lebenswelt*, the world we live in. Several times during the history of European philosophy, this inner *telos* or direction inspired by the Greeks got distorted or lost, but even when it did, it was still there implicitly, waiting to

---

results'. (Quoted by Herbert Spiegelberg in *Journal of the British Society for Phenomenology*, Vol. 1, No. 1, January 1970.)

In 1927, his work was given a new twist (in a way that proved intensely distasteful to Husserl himself) by Heidegger in *Being and Time*. Heidegger applied phenomenology to the world of everyday subjective experience of what he calls *Dasein*, that phrase including human beings amongst other things. In France, Husserl's work was transformed from a study of essence to a study of existence by Sartre and later Merleau-Ponty.

The classical introduction is Herbert Spiegelberg's *The Phenomenological Movement: An Historical Introduction* (2 vols., Nijhoff, The Hague, 1964). Individual studies on Husserl which are technically helpful are Paul Ricoeur's *Husserl: An Analysis of his Phenomenology* (Northwestern University Press, Evanston, 1967) and Edo Pivčevič's *Husserl and Phenomenology* (Hutchinson, 1970). There exists no study, as far as I know, which is genuinely comprehensible to the layman – perhaps this is not surprising in view of Husserl's own difficulties in expressing what he meant, which he also changed and developed from year to year. There is no definitive account of phenomenology, no general agreement on terms, nor could there ever be. It is a subject in development, everyone making of it what he will for his own work. The insight has been fruitful, the doctrine remains a challenge.

be found by some thinker prepared to reflect radically enough.

At one particular moment in the story, something went very badly wrong, so wrong indeed that it has not been understood or corrected even yet. That moment was the seventeenth century, and the men who really twisted the entire venture out of shape, perhaps irrevocably, were Galileo and Descartes. Their effect was at once so brilliant and so malign, that the whole of Western philosophy is still suffering from the split which they inaugurated. Objectivism reigns undisputed, and whole areas of reality, including those of the world of the senses, of affectivity, of subjectivity, of perspectival reality, of adequate psychology, all remain unknown, untreated and despised.

Objectivism, the reigning climate of mechanical–scientific objectivity, takes its start and its general justification from the procedure of Galileo. Galileo 'mathematized' nature – an exhilarating achievement and the breakthrough towards the modern science we are familiar with. But this 'mathematization' of nature, this achievement of objective knowledge through abstraction, carried along dangers with it – dangers of which Galileo, of course, inebriated with the success and possibilities of his method, could not remotely have foreseen.

First of all, Galileo *shears away* the entire world of sense-impressions, emotions, and all the realities that make up our everyday world. Then, he *substitutes* a knowledge of the mathematical properties of the world for that complete, total human world that we knew before, and counts himself richer by the exchange. Indeed his contempt for what he calls 'secondary qualities' has become famous. In fact, he carries out a double retreat from the totality: first from the totality of lived experience, and then from the totality of knowledge as such.

'All this *pure* mathematics has to do with bodies and the bodily world only through an abstraction,' writes Husserl.* But what of the world as we *experience* it, the world in which 'bodies' are perceived as coloured, resinous, gritty, smelly, dry, pleasant and so on? 'These qualities, and everything that makes up the concreteness of the sensibly intuited world, must count as manifestations of an "objective" world,' Husserl insists.† There was, in Galileo's work,

the surreptitious substitution of the mathematically substructed world of idealities for the only real world, the one that is actually given through perception, that is ever experienced and experienceable – our everyday life-world. This substitution was promptly passed on to his successors, the physicists of all the succeeding centuries.‡

In fact, Galileo, compounded his felony: he actually succeeded in substituting an abstractive picture of the real world for the world itself. He invented a 'garb of ideas' as Husserl calls it, which, when fitted over the real world, hid it completely. It was a kind of conjuring trick. 'It is through the garb of ideas that we take for *true being* what is actually a *method*.'§ In other words, Galileo substitutes mathematical abstraction for the totality of the real world in a kind of shorthand, and doesn't either notice or regret the loss.

This was the moment in European thinking when the

* *The Crisis of European Sciences and Transcendental Phenomenology*, translated by David Carr, Northwestern University Press, Evanston, 1970, p. 29.
† ibid., p. 33.
‡ ibid., pp. 48-9.
§ ibid., p. 51.

totality of our lived world got so violently raped, robbed of all its being, reality and meaning by the subtraction from it of all that had previously linked man to his own science. And on this question of reducing the real world to a mathematical picture of it, Descartes was quick and happy to add his influence. Geometry alone is the key to knowledge, and the world of the senses, of subjectivity, is nothing 'clear and distinct' at all, that is to say, nothing respectable:

> With regard to light, colours, sounds, odours, tastes, heat, cold and the other tactile qualities, they are thought with so much obscurity and confusion, that I cannot determine even whether they are true or false; in other words, whether or not the ideas I have of these qualities are in truth the ideas of real objects.*

Rather than give this world of sense-impressions the benefit of the doubt (as material for a future science, even if not the privileged geometric one) Descartes consigns it, as Galileo had done, to the refuse-heap, and there it has lain ever since.

Husserl, in *Crisis*, is trying to open up the whole subject of the totality again, trying to re-introduce that multiple and non-quantifiable subjective world again as the concern of objectivity. Husserl frets and strains under the impoverishing limits and embargoes of contemporary scientific rationalism, insisting that there can be no adequate objectivity until these two halves of our divided rationality are rejoined again.

The major missing element, the element that Husserl tries to re-locate before that wider analysis can be begun, is subjectivity. Descartes, it appears, committed a sin of

---

* Descartes, *Third Meditation*, Everyman's Library, 1960, p. 103.

omission and a sin of commission. Not only did he leave the entire world of sense-experience out of his philosophy, but he opened up the possibility of a genuine subjectivity in philosophy and then bungled the whole affair.

By failing to go deeply enough into his own newly discovered *Cogito*, by refusing the hurdle of subjectivity and thus opening up the existence of the subjective world as a problem for philosophy, Descartes remained blind to one half of the problems he himself raises with his *Cogito*. He refuses to discuss himself as embodied subject, his affective relation to the world, the questions of perspectives and the all important matter of how the world is built up inter-subjectively. All this he refuses to touch, shying away from the experience of his own subjectivity and building barriers between it and himself by his dualistic primitivism.

Descartes then, is 'the primal founder not only of the modern idea of objectivistic rationalism but also of the transcendental motif which explodes it'.* There are two Descartes. The two halves of his thinking move off independently through history, never to be re-united. Descartes is 'the starting point of two lines of development, rationalism and empiricism'.† This is natural enough because Descartes never saw the implications of his own discoveries. He made one or two tentative steps towards subjectivity, and then drew back. (For this reason alone, Husserl, at the same time he was writing *Crisis*, had to write Descartes' *Meditations* again for him!) And objectivism, having got off to a flying start, has never looked back. It has lost the deeper meaning that holds it in place as part of the total enterprise of man and functions auto-

* Husserl, op. cit., p. 73.
† ibid., p. 83.

nomously, in more or less total ignorance of its place in the scheme of things.

Since European thinking has split in this radical way, it is evident that adequate objectivity is in abeyance. We have lost the idea of the *totality* of knowledge and of endeavour, and we even seem to have lost the desire or the courage to look for it again. Whole areas of subjective experience have never been made the subject of a suitably subjective investigation by objectivity, and the reigning objectivism ignores what it cannot quantify, today as it did in the time of Galileo and Descartes. B. F. Skinner is quite explicit about it: we can only know what we can measure.

The historical origin of our present impoverishment, and the actual situation of behaviourist and positivist naïveté today, are inextricably mixed, the second taking its inspiration and its justification from the first. At the present time, it is evident that objectivity is not objective and subjectivity has hardly even been mapped out as a proper area of investigation.

Husserl emerges as a major philosopher of the totality and of the subjective in the second part of his book. He objects to objectivity subjectively, on two grounds. The first we might call ethical (he feels we have a duty to the hidden or lost *telos* to regain the *meaning* of our own science and philosophy), and the second we might call scientific, in the sense that he has intuitively grasped the necessity of a total revaluation of our *paradigms* of thinking.* We need to start asking new questions, and re-orient the whole field of inquiry such that what we most urgently need to find out about is: ourselves as subjective beings in a world that we build up inter-subjectively. In

* I refer again to the work of T. S. Kuhn, *The Structure of Scientific Revolutions*, University of Chicago Press, 1962.

fact, *Crisis* opens up a whole new science, the science of subjectivity.

Let us direct our attention to the fact that in general the world, or, rather, objects are not merely pregiven to us all in such a way that we simply have them as the substrates of their properties but that we become conscious of them ... through subjective manners of appearance, or manners of givenness, without noticing it in particular; in fact we are for the most part not even aware of it at all. Let us now shape this into a new universal direction of interest; let us establish a consistent universal interest in the 'how' of the manners of givenness ... that is, with our interest exclusively and constantly directed toward *how*, throughout the alteration of relative validities, subjective appearances, and opinions, the coherent, universal validity *world – the* world – comes into being for us.*

T. S. Kuhn writes of revolutionary science – those manners of rethinking the whole field of scientific effort and interest which suddenly galvanize the whole scientific world into interest and controversy, and end up by reorganizing the basic and accepted paradigm of thinking. Revolutionary science suddenly allows of an explanation of something which traditional science has broken its teeth on, and before which it sits, humiliated and defeated. Revolutionary science suddenly makes everything possible again, by inviting people to look at the same phenomena from a totally different angle. May not Husserl's suggestion be such a revolutionary scientific idea? Would not his plan, if successful, make sense of a great many phenomena which, for us at the moment, remain unexplained and in total darkness?

For Husserl's new suggestion is revolutionary in Kuhn's sense. It reverses (and is conscious of reversing) three centuries of paradigms. By a return to the subjectively

* ibid., p. 144.

experienced world, that objectivism established so firmly by Galileo and Descartes could re-think itself in terms of a more comprehensive set of criteria. Since so much has got lost on the way, it is in our interests to look again at the presuppositions which debar us from making use of our own philosophy. The *telos* of the whole enterprise has got lost, and only by a return to the *totality* can it be re-gained:

Among the objects of the life-world we also find human beings, with all their human action and concern, works and suffering, living in common in the world-horizon in their particular social interrelations.... All this, too, then, shall be included as we carry out our new universal direction of interest. A coherent theoretical interest shall now be directed exclusively toward the universe of the subjective.*

In that universe, we shall study the 'overlapping horizon validities', the 'corroborating verifications' we make of each other's interpretations of the world, or the 'refuting cancellings-out' which we operate where they do not fit in with what seems to everyone else in the world to be the case. The inter-relation of worlds is a vast new subject, which has never been treated scientifically, i.e. objectively, before.

The world is thus *replaced*. It is not the spatial support of mathematically known extensions, but a world of inter-acting subjectivities which belongs to people, which they confer *meaning* upon and *control* through their conferring meaning upon it. One major job which could be carried out would be a systematic investigation of the cultural setting and cultural achievement of science and scientists in our world, as a set of subjective attitudes, in-

* ibid., p. 146.

volvements and prejudices.* Since our concern is to be with the totality and with the perspectival world of our counter-subjects in our societies, the value and meaning we accord to science will be very much a matter of our own choice, our own 'intentionality' as Husserl would say. It depends, that is to say, what meaning we *confer* upon scientific activity. At the moment, we confer virtually no coherent meaning at all, and thus objectivism reigns in place of an adequate objectivity. This inquiry into the world-validity of scientific activity would be one of the first tasks of the new subjective attitude.

There is no method for beginning:

As is the case with all undertakings which are new in principle, for which not even an analogy can serve as guide, this beginning takes place with a certain unavoidable naïveté.... We wish, then, to consider the surrounding life-world concretely, in its neglected relativity and according to all the manners of relativity belonging essentially to it.... Our exclusive task shall be to comprehend precisely this style, precisely this whole merely subjective and apparently incomprehensible 'Heraclitean flux'.†

Husserl takes as his guiding idea, his major instrument

* ibid., pp. 135-7. The view that science is an interested and subjective option or wager has been advanced before, notably by E. A. Burtt in *The Metaphysical Foundations of Modern Physical Science* (Routledge & Kegan Paul, 2nd edn, 1932). Burtt's chapters on Galileo and Descartes are particularly illuminating. T. S. Kuhn has shown, more recently, that the choice of a paradigm is a kind of commitment in the scientific community. Michael Polanyi's distinction, in *Personal Knowledge* (Routledge & Kegan Paul, 2nd edn, 1962), between 'focal' and 'subsidiary' knowledge is also relevant. Burtt, Husserl, Kuhn and Polanyi set up a kind of epistemological square. In that square lies our problem, and its challenge to our objectivity.

† ibid., p. 156.

of investigation, the notion of *perspectives*, of a *perspectival world*.

The objects in the world are seen from different perspectives. We move round them, seeing them and experiencing them in different modalities, while other people in the world do the same. We are all conscious that there is only one world, but we are also quite sure that we all see it differently, we all interpret it differently, and we all attribute different meanings to it at various times. The world is a communalized set of perspectives. Nothing is ever fixed, everything is subject to the meaning *we* give to it.* 'Thus in general the world exists not only for isolated men but for the community of men; and this is due to the fact that even what is straightforwardly perceptual is communalized.'†

We are all, in fact, quite at home in our interpreted world: 'Each individual ... has different aspects, different sides, perspectives, etc. ... but in each case these are taken from the same total system of multiplicities of which each individual is constantly conscious.'‡

But the difficulty consists in bringing to consciousness, to explicit formulation, what we all know instinctively and through common sense. Husserl puts it in an extreme way so that we have to reckon with his seriousness: '*Anything that is – whatever its meaning and to whatever region it belongs – is an index of a subjective system of correlations.*'§ This we might all be said to be *aware of*, without being able to say that we *know* anything about it. And it is this basic ignorance (not unawareness) of the total relativity of the appearance-patterns of our counter-subjects in the world which necessitates the return to a total subjective inquiry:

* ibid., pp. 163-4.   ‡ ibid., p. 164.

† ibid., p. 163.   § ibid., p. 165.

Subjective Objections to 'Objectivity'

The fact which is naïvely taken for granted, that each person sees things and the world in general as they appear to him, concealed, as we now realize, a great horizon of remarkable truths whose uniqueness and systematic interconnection never entered the philosophical purview. The correlation between world ... and its subjective manners of givenness never evoked philosophical wonder ... in spite of the fact that it had made itself felt even in pre-Socratic philosophy and among the Sophists – though here only as a motive for sceptical argumentation. This correlation never aroused a philosophical interest of its own which could have made it the object of an appropriate scientific attitude. Philosophers were confined by what was taken for granted, i.e., that each thing appeared differently in each case to each person.*

In a remarkable flash-back to the Greeks, Husserl indicates a missed basic insight. It was missed at the moment when Plato simply dismissed Protagoras instead of truly engaging with what was implied in Protagoras's position. As if trying to re-constitute what Protagoras was really trying to say (instead of what Plato took him to be saying), Husserl goes on:

Everything thus stands in correlation with its own manners of givenness ... and everything has its modes of validity and its particular manners of synthesis.... No matter where we turn, every entity that is valid for me and every conceivable subject as existing in actuality is thus correlatively ... an index of its systematic multiplicities.†

How is it 'systematic'? What way have we of classifying sets of subjective constructions about the world? What way have we of comparing the consistency (or 'style') of a way of seeing the world, say mine, and comparing it with some other person's, say yours?

* loc. cit.   † ibid., p. 166.

Towards Deep Subjectivity

As soon as one has progressed far enough ... to see the purely subjective in its own self-enclosed pure context as intentionality and to recognize it as the function of forming ontic meaning, the theoretical interest grows quickly, and one becomes more astonished at each step by the endless array of emerging problems and important discoveries to be made.*

There is no mystery about the idea of 'intentionality'. It refers to our power of conferring meaning. The consistent way I operate my intentionality, the consistent way, that is, that I confer meaning, according to certain shapes and necessities (which after a while become predictable) offers the interpreter of the subjective world his first vital clue. With this attention to the 'intentionality' of subjects in the world (the way they confer meaning and interpret their world) the massive task of re-integrating subjectivity into objective research has begun.

Intentionality (the purely subjective) is, so to speak, a hypothesis. I operate a sort of spatial supposition, I 'intend' what I see, hear, smell, want, fear, etc., in a certain manner. This 'intentionality' is thus open to others in the world to confirm or disconfirm.

Once we have realized the connections between subjectivity as intentionality and the role of intentionality in bringing my world into being and cancelling it out again in a series of infinitely fast 'inspired guesses', we arrive at the point where we have to turn the objective hypothesis round 180 degrees and observe the subjectivity we are studying, not as a body operated upon by forces in a mechanical world, but as a freely emitting centre of meanings. We attain a point of vantage from where we find out that we are *conferring* meaning upon the world instead of letting the world shove its meanings down over us. We

* ibid., p. 169.

become *active* in forming 'ontic' decisions, that is to say decisions about the being of things, instead of accepting the usual objective paradigm of Lockean *tabula rasa* or some kind of behaviourist–Pavlovian conditioned reflex assumption.

And even modern research into the brain and its manners of receiving information, especially through the eyes, seems to confirm Husserl's revolutionary thesis. We do in fact more or less 'process' what we see at the retinal level. What is finally sent along to the brain as information has been heavily processed at the retina, and a sort of temporary hypothesis about what the eye is seeing is transmitted rather than any direct information about what there is 'out there'. The idea of a retinal hypothesis in fact is only a biological–physiological form of Husserl's basic insight: that we confer meaning upon the world by the use of what he calls 'intentionality' and thus, in a sense, create a world all the time, in a series of rapid achievements. These achievements are going on in everyone else too, all the time, and when the series of hypothetical achievements going on in A and in B criss-cross, the inter-subjective world is called into being, and the world of perspectives is set up automatically. Neither A nor B sees 'the reality', but both have their 'version' of the reality, both thus confer 'ontic' meanings and significances upon what is experienced, and thus the world of total subjective relativity is created.

'Are we not also doing science? Are we not establishing truths about true being? Are we not entering upon the dangerous road of double truth? Can there be, next to objective truth, yet a second truth, the subjective?'* Husserl is fully conscious of the dangers of the task: he is sure objectivity will obstruct as much as it can, but it is

* ibid., p. 175.

not really that which worries him so much as the totally exposed nature of the enterprise itself, the fact that it has no formed and formulable *method* to vaunt in an objective world: 'Immediately we become involved in great difficulties, in unexpected and at first insoluble paradoxes, which place our whole undertaking in question.'* For 'no objective truth, whether in the prescientific or the scientific sense, i.e., no claim about objective being, ever enters our sphere of scientific discipline, whether as a premise or as a conclusion'.†

In fact, the method which Husserl proposes is the use of the 'bracketing' process developed in his own earlier philosophy.‡ But we do not need to adopt that method as our own. Indeed, it has yet to prove itself and its powers. Husserl's delineation of the *problem of subjectivity* is of vital importance, however, in defining a new and adequate objectivity. He proposes that we pay attention to the *totality*. But the method is new and untried and everything remains to be done:

Its beginning course ... is necessarily one of experiencing and thinking in naïve self-evidence. It possesses no formed logic and methodology in advance and can achieve its method and even the genuine sense of its accomplishments only through ever renewed self-reflections. Its fate (understood subsequently, to be sure, as an essentially necessary one) is to become involved again and again in paradoxes, which, arising out of uninvestigated and even unnoticed horizons, remain functional and announce themselves as incomprehensibilities. §

* loc. cit.

† loc. cit.

‡ ibid., p. 181: 'The epoche ... leads us to recognize ... that the world ... takes its ontic meaning entirely from our intentional life.'

§ loc. cit.

If the world as the world we live in, the world we confer 'ontic' meanings upon and build up inter-subjectively with other people, is to be made the subject of our inquiry, then it should very precisely be made the subject of our inquiry and not the object. 'One must finally achieve the insight that no objective science, no matter how exact, explains or ever can explain anything in a serious sense.'* Strong words coming from one who had spent his whole life as a mathematician and logician. Yet they indicate the seriousness of the problem as Husserl sees it, and as he presents it as a subjective objection to the prevailing objectivity: this is revolutionary science in Kuhn's sense – and it points to the possibility of an achieved and adequate objectivity. The fact that the problem has been posed by Husserl at all testifies to the process of deep subjectivity at work in his thinking.

Since in his effort to re-integrate subjectivity as meaning-conferring into objectivity, Husserl has been forced to suspend temporarily all belief in the actual contents or importance of the sciences, it is not surprising that we have to come back pretty rapidly to their empirical existence in the world and attempt to work out a viable attitude towards them. For the physical and mental sciences of prevalent objectivity are *there*, towering over us, and we have the interim job of discovering what we should do about them.

Subjectivity itself thus turns out to be, not only an intentionality, a meaning-conferring ability, but a relationship. It is (I think) impossible to have an objective relationship to anything at all: at the very least it would be intentional, and thus subjective, even if it were relatively passionless, like my relation to the pillar-box. It does not

* ibid., p. 189.

move me to strong feelings about it, but I have decided all the same that it is red.

What relationship, then, can we have to objective facts, to the sciences, to the prevailing quantitative paradigm of the world we live in?

What relationship can I have to the following facts? The American aircraft carrier *Saratoga* has a striking force of 108 planes. She weighs 70,000 tons, she is 346 metres long, she carries 4,500 men of whom 750 are concerned with aviation. She can sail at 33 knots. From her four take-off strips 40 planes can be catapulted in 5 minutes. She has four super-rapid lifts linking the deck to the hangar of 25,000 square metres which can hold 108 planes. The destructive power of these planes is higher than that of 1,000 Flying Fortresses of the Second World War.*

These are what objectivity would call the 'facts' about the *Saratoga*. They imply further 'facts' about the world, about the Mediterranean, about the Russian presence in the Mediterranean and so on.

Yet what is my relation to these facts? I already have an intentional relation (one of vague foreboding and unease) and it is doubtful that I could ever have an objective relation to these facts. Since it would seem, then, that I must be related to these facts, *somehow*, subjectively, in what way can I be related to them?

It is in this context that the philosophy of subjectivity of Søren Kierkegaard is of particular usefulness. For he has analysed the various modes in which I can be related to facts, to objectivity, to 'System' generally.

There would seem to be two *directions* of relationship. I can direct myself entirely towards the objectivity of the facts, or I can direct my attention back towards myself

* *Paris Match*, 5 September 1970.

as being in connection with these facts:

> For an objective reflection the truth becomes an object, something objective, and thought must be pointed away from the subject. For a subjective reflection the truth becomes a matter of appropriation, of inwardness, of subjectivity, and thought must probe more and more deeply into the subject and his subjectivity.*

Subjectivity for Kierkegaard is not the same thing as it is for Husserl, nor what I mean by deep subjectivity, though all three notions overlap. But Kierkegaard's philosophy of subjectivity, as he develops it in the *Postscript*, does enlarge Husserl's conception of subjectivity as meaning-conferring (intentionality) by integrating subjectivity directly into the ethical sphere, where it becomes *choice*, relationship, responsibility. Meaning-conferring is no longer a matter of epistemology, nor of a subjective science, however thorough. For Kierkegaard, we are related subjectively to the world and have to choose significantly in it. Husserl's concept of subjectivity emphasized that meaning-conferring is an active process, and Kierkegaard now opens up the new dimension for us, that subjectivity is inescapably *ethical* meaning-conferring, is, in fact, choice: commitment or rejection. By taking a step back into history (the *Postscript*, 1846, ante-dates Husserl's *Crisis* by about ninety years), we take a conceptual step forward. Husserl's meaning becomes more clear, not less so, in the Kierkegaardian light.

The way of objective reflection leads to abstract thought, to mathematics, to historical knowledge of different kinds; and always it leads away from the subject, whose existence

---

* *Concluding Unscientific Postscript*, translated by D. F. Swenson and W. Lowrie, Princeton University Press, 1941, p. 171.

or non-existence, and from the objective point of view quite rightly, becomes infinitely indifferent.*

Kirkegaard, like Husserl, makes a subjective objection to objectivity, though the objectivity involved in the two cases is, of course, historically different. The objectivity which provoked Kierkegaard's ire was the so-called philosophical objectivity of the Hegelian System, which prided itself on starting from no assumptions or presuppositions at all. Feeling rightly incensed by this illogical, indeed meaningless, claim, Kierkegaard erects an entire philosophy of subjectivity which takes a definite and explicit presupposition as its starting point: it is, that the individual thinker is the ultimate ethical (and religious) reality and that the whole of objectivity has finally to be judged and evaluated by him. (It is very close to Husserl's project of a 'suspension' of the objective sciences.) Since ethical and religious reality is the final reality, indeed the only reality that concerns the individual if one takes the matter deep enough, then the status of objectivity in the world was not, for Kierkegaard, a very impressive one.

'The only reality that exists for an existing individual is his own ethical reality. To every other reality he stands in a cognitive relation; but true knowledge consists in translating the real into the possible.'† With this elegant academic joke, Kierkegaard poses (for us as it were) the question of our personal relationship to the 'facts' about the *Saratoga*. There is no doubt that the 'facts' are 'the real' – but how are we, how am I, how are you, personally, to 'translate the real into the possible'? How are we to *deploy* 'reality', which future 'possibility' shall we give it? In that decision, in that meaning-conferring activity,

* ibid., p. 173.
† ibid., p. 280.

Kierkegaard poses us the question about the *status* of knowledge, objective knowledge, in the world: 'In pure thought we are over our ears in profundity, and yet there is something rather absent-minded about it all, because the pure thinker is not clear about what it means to be a human being.'*

'The existing individual who really exists,' says Kierkegaard, 'thinks everything in relation to himself, being infinitely interested in existing. Socrates was thus a man whose energies were devoted to thinking; but he reduced all other knowledge to indifference in that he infinitely accentuated ethical knowledge.'† Kierkegaard implies that this is the only adequate and correct attitude to knowledge. All objective knowledge is the servant of the use we intend to make of it. And the use we make of it necessarily involves us as ethical beings, therefore the fundamental study of the truly existing thinker is to work out a relationship between objective knowledge, science and so on – and himself as ethically responsible and meaning-conferring ultimate reality.

Kierkegaard, it must be admitted, has really very little use for objective knowledge at all. His aim in the *Postscript* is to prove that, with reference to religion and Christianity, subjectivity is truth. Consequently, all other forms of truth, all the endeavours of science and so on, get drastically downgraded. From the Socratic point of view (which is of course his own), he asserts, all other knowledge than knowledge of existence is 'accidental, its scope and degree a matter of indifference'.‡

But we don't have to be concerned with religious truth, in Kierkegaard's emphatic sense, to see the relevance of

* loc. cit.
† ibid., p. 281.
‡ ibid., p. 183.

his analysis of subjectivity to our own inquiries into what possible relationship we can have to objectivity. Shear away the explicitly religious dimension, substitute 'objectivity' for 'Hegel' throughout, and the Kierkegaardian. philosophy of subjectivity is directly relevant to our own inquiry. His objection to objectivity is a subjective one, coming as it does from a passionate involvement with the ethical responsibility of the thinking individual.

'In the principle that subjectivity, inwardness, is the truth, there is comprehended the Socratic wisdom, whose everlasting merit it was to have become aware of the essential significance of existence, of the fact that the knower is an existing individual.'* As a 'knower' and as an 'existing individual', I have my work cut out to arrive at the right conclusion every time. But anything less than complete success in *this*, is to have failed utterly, to know *anything*. The minimum demand, as far as Kierkegaard is concerned, is to be absolutely right every time. This is only possible if the existing individual soaks and saturates his sense of what 'knowledge' is, in his sense of ethical responsibility for it – he personally.

'What is abstract thought? It is thought without a thinker.'† That is the nub of the matter. Thinkerless thought is mere objectivity – it is a failure of responsibility.

All knowledge which does not inwardly relate itself to existence, in the reflection of inwardness, is, essentially viewed, accidental knowledge; its degree and scope is essentially indifferent.... Knowledge has a relationship to the knower, who is essentially an existing individual, and ... for this reason all essential knowledge is essentially related to existence. Only ethical and ethico-religious knowledge has an essential relationship to the existence of the knower.‡

* loc. cit.   † ibid., p. 296.   ‡ ibid., pp. 176-7.

Subjective Objections to 'Objectivity'

An achievement in physics or biology, Kierkegaard would argue, is itself neutral. It is the real but, so far, it is *only* the real. All its possibilities lie before it. But since true knowledge consists in translating the real into the possible, the question then arises: what are we to do with this achievement in positive science? What 'possible' future shall we direct it towards?

Political use of science, for instance, has its irrational (objective but not adequately objective) underside. Until I know what use is going to be made of what is discovered by objectivity, the scientific achievement itself remains of merely academic interest. In translating the real into the possible, objective science and objective military strategy might very well fail to be rational. The success of a technique is, in its deployment, capable of being a failure of adequate objectivity.

What can I make of these 'facts', for instance?:

Expanded Chemical Warfare: The Air Force has told Congress that it will spend $70·8 million on 10 million gallons of chemicals used for Vietnam defoliation and crop-killing in the fiscal year beginning 1 July, a $24·9 million increase over this year's figure. Next year's expanded efforts are in line with the continuing increase in the U.S. chemical warfare programme in Vietnam. In the first nine months of 1967, 843,606 acres in Vietnam were drenched with defoliants and 121,400 acres with crop-killing chemicals, a figure which slightly exceeded the totals for the whole of 1966.*

Chomsky quotes again from *Science* of 10 May 1968.

* Quoted by Noam Chomsky in *American Power and the New Mandarins*, Penguin Books, 1969, p. 254, from *Science*, American Association for the Advancement of Science, Washington DC, 24 May 1968, p. 863.

The sheer horror of the account imposes a full quotation:

> The DOD can raise the red herring of 'long-term' effects, but there can be no doubt about the short-term effects: 2,4-D and 2,4,5-T kill the green vegetation. When followed by fire bombs, the dead foliage and twigs burn, as they did on some 100,000 acres (about 40,000 hectares) in the 'Iron Triangle' last spring.
>
> Through the simple process of starvation, a land without green foliage will quickly become a land without insects, without birds, without animal life of any form. News photographs and on-the-spot descriptions indicate that some areas have been sprayed repeatedly to assure a complete kill of the vegetation. There can be no doubt that the DOD is, in the short run, going beyond mere genocide to biocide. It commandeered the entire U.S. production of 2,4,5-T for 1967 and 1968 [some 13 to 14 million pounds (6·36 million kilos) according to U.S. Tariff Commission reports]. If one combines this with other chemicals the DOD concedes it is using, there is a sufficient amount to kill 97 per cent of the above-ground vegetation on over 10 million acres of land (about 4 million hectares) – an area so big that it would require over sixty years for a man to walk on each acre.
>
> The long-term effects of spraying such an area may be imponderable, but the short-term effects of using these chemicals are certain: a lot of leaves, trees, rice plants, and other vegetation are dead or dying; and a lot of insects, birds, animals, and a few humans have either migrated or died of starvation. The North Vietnamese are fortunate – they have only bombs to contend with.*

Chomsky's book raises once more, and this time in an acute form, the question of the status of 'facts' *vis-à-vis* objectivity – the prevalent or ruling objectivity. Chomsky's book is packed full of facts. But there is no

* ibid., p. 255.

fact which is free of a moral bearing or implication. There is no fact to which we can, as readers, stand in an objective relationship.

The facts about chemical warfare alone, as quoted above, are enough to cause a kind of short-circuit in our sense of what is objective. For if the facts which Chomsky quotes are facts, why do those facts continue to be facts? Surely a simple perusal of them is enough to convince one of the total irrationality of what is presented as objectivity (whether it be claimed as strategic, ideological or political necessity)? But no. What are facts of horror to the ordinary human being are facts of objective necessity for the American administration.

Facts obviously have a *modality* and are *different* according to the perspective from which we view them. Seen from where Chomsky sees them, the facts of the Vietnam war amount to war crimes, if not crimes against humanity, totally un-objective and quite indefensible. ('There can be no doubt that the DOD is, in the short run, going beyond mere genocide to biocide.') Seen from the Pentagon, the 'same' facts seem to be objective and strategic necessities.

But are they the 'same' facts? Husserl has suggested that we go into the business of intentionality, of meaning-conferring, and it would be profitable indeed to examine the subjective structures of American strategic thinking as a meaning-conferring activity. It would certainly be profitable to examine the structures of meaning-conferring as subjective constructions, as 'cultural achievements' as Husserl put it, and then compare these structures with the structures of those who live in Vietnam – even up to and including the U.S. Army and Air Force who carry out the spraying operations. This three-part convergence on the 'facts' of chemical spraying in Vietnam would open up whole vistas of unexamined and malignant aspects of received objectivity.

It might also provoke us, at last, to ask ourselves what 'a fact' is – whether there is any such thing. Can we ever. 'appeal to the facts'? The 'appeal' itself is a meaning-conferring activity and sets up a subjective relationship between myself and the fact to which I appeal – I need it. My opponent may 'appeal' to the same 'fact'. What is common to the two cases may simply be the appeal.

Noam Chomsky's book on Vietnam emerges as the historical successor to the philosophies of concern of Husserl and Kierkegaard. Chomsky, himself admirably objective where his science demands it, yet knows, like Kierkegaard, that he has a duty to knowledge which exceeds the demands of the academic and professional world. He feels the necessity to move beyond a 'merely cognitive' relation to his knowledge, and to establish knowledge in an ethical relationship to the life-world. Chomsky finds himself constrained to insist that there are limits beyond which objectivity may not presume to pass:

By entering into the arena of argument and counter-argument, of technical feasibility and tactics, of footnotes and citations, by accepting the presumption of legitimacy of debate on certain issues, one has already lost one's humanity. This is the feeling I find almost impossible to repress when going through the motions of building a case against the American war in Vietnam. Anyone who puts a fraction of his mind to the task can construct a case that is overwhelming; surely this is now obvious.*

No, it is not obvious. Objectivity is still far from convinced. It has *its* 'facts', *its* perspectives, *its* meaning-conferring activities. Chomsky, in citing the official facts from *Science*, doesn't cause objectivity to recognize the *mod-*

* ibid., pp. 11-12.

ality of those very facts. All 'facts' have modalities (ways they can be used or cited) and all modalities imply ambiguities. Objectivity stoutly refuses to recognize this in any shape or form.

And, of course, Chomsky's book is another subjective objection to objectivity, and much of it is an inquiry into objectivity and logic, as they are understood, and as they ought to be understood. The book is an exercise in deep subjectivity and shows that the combination of objective study of perspectives and personal ethical commitment to the task in hand, is a possibility. Engaged writing does not preclude adequately objective writing, though it may permit itself to be subjective towards objectivity. And Chomsky is aware, as Lorenz and others are, of the behavioural attitude underlying the American objectivity, at home and in Vietnam:

Obviously, one must learn from social and behavioural science whatever one can; obviously, these fields should be pursued in as serious a way as is possible. But it will be quite unfortunate, and highly dangerous, if they are not accepted and judged on their merits and according to their actual, not pretended, accomplishments.... To anyone who has any familiarity with the social and behavioural sciences (or the 'policy sciences') the claim that there are certain considerations and principles too deep for the outsider to comprehend is simply an absurdity, unworthy of comment.*

Chomsky, as a deeply subjective, that is to say as an ethically subjective, thinker, is concerned very precisely to 'place' the objective attitudes and sciences of his society, and establish their bounds of competence and validity. It is perhaps not surprising that Chomsky should end up with a position not very far from Husserl's remark

* ibid., p. 271.

that: 'One must finally achieve the insight that no objective science, no matter how exact, explains or ever can explain anything in a serious sense.' Chomsky himself writes, in a very similar spirit: 'The social and be-. havioural studies should be seriously studied not only for their intrinsic interest, but so that the student can be made quite aware of exactly how little they have to say about the problems of man and society that really matter.'* This is entirely in the spirit of Kierkegaard, and opens up a whole new range of intellectual possibilities and attitudes which are not simply obedient to objectivity in a behavioural sense. Chomsky sweeps straight on from this point in his text to a whole series of subjective and ethical questions, and ends his peroration thus: 'If American intellectuals will be preoccupied with such questions as these, they can have an invaluable civilizing influence on society and on the schools. If, as is more likely, they regard them with disdain as mere sentimental nonsense, then our children will have to look elsewhere for enlightenment and guidance.'† As Kierkegaard would have put it, Either – Or.

It is a grim Either – Or that Chomsky poses. For the likelihood of its being taken up and accepted as a genuinely objective challenge, by objectivity, is so diminishingly small, and one can feel the hopelessness of the situation even as one reads Chomsky's lines – a hopelessness he must himself have felt when writing them.

Nevertheless, it remains an Either – Or, and what is at stake is an adequate objectivity. One does not begin by creating a whole new apparatus of technical terms and methods by which we could 'analyse' the situation in some distorted spirit of 'disinterested scholarship'. We have to approach not the technical and behavioural as-

*ibid., p. 253.   †ibid., p. 254.

pects of our knowledge, but their moral bearing and meaning, and for this one needs no tools or experimental
equipment at all. The fact that one doesn't need any
quantitative laboratory equipment to carry out the basic
research that Chomsky indicates as a first necessity probably means that objectivity will never face the problem
of adequately objective knowledge at all, and so 'our
children will have to look elsewhere for enlightenment and
guidance'. Where might that be? Certainly the Pentagon
should be interested in *that* possibility – directly brought
about by its own refusal to examine the moral implications of its own objectivity.

Subjective objection to objectivity is not a quantitative
matter but a qualitative one. It involves the thinking mind
as responsible being. The exercise of deep subjectivity
consists in dragging back, tirelessly and without losing
hope, the dominant objectivity to a point where it is
quite evidently the issues that concern us as human beings
in the life-world that we are concerned to discuss first
and to discuss constantly.

What deep subjectivity constellates for us, what it
opens up as a possibility for us, is *adequacy*.

Apart from the world of the senses, seventeenth-cen-
tury rationalism left one other vital element out of
its philosophy: the thinker himself. Remorselessly, the
thinker was excluded from what he thought. Nothing
except his pure presence as thinking mind was allowed
to stand. Everything that belonged to him as an ethical
being was swept out with the 'secondary qualities' and
refused re-entry.

It was not the thinker as rationalist mathematician who
was swept out, of course, but the whole man, the thinker
as a human being endowed with sensitivity, personality,

commitments and so on. Since the world could only be adequately described *more geometrico*, it followed that affectivity was ruthlessly excluded from consideration.

But this objectivity was an *ignis fatuus*, a dream, a fantasy. European man had fallen madly in love with his excluded self. He was inebriated by the idea of impersonal knowledge. This became so much of an ideal for him (a 'paradigm') that he became incapable of *thinking* outside it at all. Indeed, he did not even want to do so. Exclusiveness, not inclusiveness, was his aim.

But adequacy stands in danger if the thinker is left out of his own philosophical line of argument to this extent. Unless the thinker is to some extent humanly responsible for his own line of reasoning, the whole idea of an adequately thought out philosophy is menaced.

Descartes' determination, for instance, to exclude the world of subjectivity from scientific discussion on the grounds that is *unquantifiable, and therefore intractable*, amounts to a refusal to consider the whole problem. Descartes decided to consider only selected bits of the problem. Since he has so limited his aim, it is not surprising that he should achieve a certain amount of success.

But it is beginning to appear as if, today, the refusal to treat of the *totality* of problems is itself a failure of adequate objectivity. To put it in a strenuous form: to be adequate today is to refuse to deal with less than the whole problem or problems, of which no part may be quantifiable at any stage of the inquiry.

This is to step up the level of adequacy considerably beyond what Descartes modestly set himself as an aim. It may look too ambitious, but it is in fact the *minimum* demand that modern thinking can make. Adequacy as it must now be defined (in face of the kind of demand that Chomsky, for instance, makes of us) is the study of the *totality* of problems, objective and subjective, by the *whole* thinker, taking into account *all* the evidence, both quantifiable and unquantifiable.

What, for instance, bearing in mind the 'facts' quoted by Chomsky in *The New Mandarins*, can we still make of the self-confident rationalism of Bertrand Russell's peroration to his *Wisdom of the West*? :

> It is disinterested inquiry that is the good. This is an ethical principle that stems from Pythagoras. The pursuit of a truth which is acknowledged as independent of the seeker, this has been, from the time of Thales, the ethical driving force behind the scientific movement. *Admittedly this does leave untouched the ethical problem arising from possible uses and abuses of invention.* But while this problem must be faced, it does not help our understanding of these matters if we mix up together these quite distinct and separate issues.*

Russell states his belief reasonably and elegantly, indeed these sentiments are a fitting tribute to the great tradition he discusses in his book. Disinterested inquiry has certainly delivered the scientific goods.

Yet, even so, there is something which today rings hollow in these lines. There is a certain lack, too, in the unassailably correct position expressed in these last Russellian periods. There is a refusal of any *commitment* in the thinker, of the total involvement of thinker and his thought, involvement which may have to be 'interested' if it is to succeed at all in getting itself heard against the powerful drone of the received rationality of a given society. If Russell were entirely right, and 'disinterested inquiry' were truly (and exclusively) 'the good', why does Chomsky's *New Mandarins* have such a powerful effect upon the reader? Chomsky is felt as a powerful presence

Wisdom of the West, Macdonald, 1959, p. 313. Italics mine.

in the book, arguing from the concern of deep subjectivity a case for adequately objective understanding that, save for such involvement, would never get a hearing at all.

Russell continues:

The enquirer is thus confronted by a twofold task. On the one hand, it is his business to pursue, to the best of his powers, the independent objects of his study. He must do this regardless of whether his findings will soothe or upset. Just as ethical principles are no respecters of persons, so the results of inquiry are not bound to respect our feelings. *On the other hand, there is the problem of turning discovery to good account, in the ethical sense.**

There again is that tell-tale throw-away line at the end, which makes one uneasy for the whole position of confident optimism that is expressed in the rest. It would seem to be, today, not so much a matter of 'turning discovery to good account' as to prevent it from committing genocide, biocide and finally suicide. It is a matter not so much of promoting the best, as of averting the worst, that science can achieve.

Russell's position is still the Cartesian one, the rationalist–mathematical one, the one that has dominated our thinking for three centuries. In that world-view, the exclusion of the thinker from the thought is a prime necessity.

But such an exclusion brings up the problem of adequacy in an acute form. It may be that the thinker may no longer be excluded from the thought, if his work is to have validity in an urgent situation. Of course, all the difficulties of propounding such a view are obvious, all the distortions and prejudices which Russell so rightly fears. But those are risks it would appear we have to run.

* loc. cit. Italics mine.

For if 'the good' is to be sought today, it cannot be in a spirit of Olympian 'disinterestedness' as it could perhaps when Russell began philosophizing. Nowadays 'the good' has to be ethically 'interested', has to be deeply subjective.

None of this is to deny, of course, that Russell in his private life was deeply subjective in the sense developed in this essay. His imprisonment for pacifism in 1918, his work for limitation of nuclear weapons in the late 1950s, his presidency of the Campaign for Nuclear Disarmament in 1958, and his imprisonment for the practice of civil disobedience in 1961, all testify not only to commitment in the man himself, but also to the conscious use of his body as a sign in the manner of an indirect communication.

But he is, in philosophy, the last of the Renaissance rationalists, the last of the eighteenth-century empiricists. His belief in pure reason excludes the thinker from the thought as an *a priori* necessity. This means to say that Hegel, Kierkegaard, Heidegger, Sartre, Camus, Guevara, Marcuse are meaningless to him. They are so many woolly-minded poets. And this, in its turn, implies that the realities they write about are not realities for him. He was thus seriously out of touch with much of the ideological flow of twentieth-century history. Hippiedom he would not have seen as a form of rationality at all.

And this in its turn means that the enormous influence he has had, and has still, on the academies, is seriously disabling for them. To take refuge in Cartesian rationalism or Humean empiricism is just too easy, given the pressing complexity of the problems of today. In fact Russellian empiricism (or rationalism – whichever way one likes to look at it, for Reason is for Russell, as it was for Descartes, the only certain knowledge we can have) offers an easy escape-route for the philosophical professionals. Men as great as Russell, both in his thought and in his life, occur rarely through the centuries, and transcend their own limitations. But those who follow find in his doctrine of detachment a powerful soporific. If Russell's influence endorses a current tendency in the academies towards an inturned refusal to deal with the problems of contemporary ideology, then this influence has to be combated.

Adequate thinking now has to bear the mark of the thinker in its results. 'What is abstract thought?' asked Kierkegaard. 'It is thought without a thinker.' Can we any longer afford such abstraction?

We have to re-think the rationalistic presuppositions of the seventeenth century in order to make our own thinking adequate to the situation of today. Subjectivity as originating source of genuine philosophic concern must be allowed, openly, methodologically, as a founding reality in our inquiries. Indeed, it may already be the case that *only* those with a subjective concern for the world have a right to speak.

5

THE PERSPECTIVAL WORLD AND SUBJECTIVE METHOD

Naum Gabo's 'Spherical Theme' (1964) appears from directly in front of it to be a construction in one circular piece of metal. Only when one moves round it does it appear that there are two curved circles of metal bent and placed back to back. From a position at a ninety degree angle to one's first position, one can in fact look right through the two halves of what appeared at first to be a solid object. At forty-five degrees to one's original position, the ambiguity is perfectly established, as the rhythmic quality of the whole forbids a final decision as to whether or not the construction is in one piece.

In the art of Gabo, and in kinetic art like that of Nicolas Schöffer, we have made evident for us in aesthetic form the most basic truth of perceptual experience: that what we see is directly dependent upon the perspective from which we see it. As Schöffer's constructions turn and shimmer in front of our eyes, or as we move slowly round the complex constructions of Gabo, we see, at each new moment of our experience, a new perspective of a work which has a certain objectivity out there in space. But what that work 'is', we never know, for at any given moment we only see a part of it. If the work itself moves, or if I myself move around it, everything becomes that much more difficult to describe.

Kinetic art illustrates the fundamental problem of ethics and of politics. Everything is perspectives, all our 'truth' is a selection from perspectival reality. We never know, we can never know, anything as it is, as it might be, so to speak, in the mind of God. We 'know' selected parts and combinations of our world, we have various relations towards them and feelings towards them, and these, like the objects in the world around us, are themselves in constant movement and change. We live in a world totally relative and are ourselves relative aspects of relativity.

The cinema has been most expressive and insistent about this in recent years. Jean-Luc Godard has been very precise in posing his problem:

Here is how Juliette, at 37 minutes past 3, watched the pages moving of this object which, in the language of journalism, is called a review. And here is how, about a hundred and fifty frames further on, another young woman, '*sa semblable, sa soeur*', saw the same object. Where is the truth then? Seen full face or in profile? And first of all, what is an object?*

Within a world of fluctuating visual and sensory perspectives, I live in a kind of continual, infinitely fast, alternation between hypothesis and correction. I give provisional meanings to things and within a split second have modified those meanings in the light of further reflection, perception, instinct or discovery. Correction of

* 'Jean-Luc Godard dans la modernité', *Les temps modernes*, March 1968, p. 1567.

hypothesis is infinitely fast: I am never conscious of having carried out a correction because I am already way ahead into the next hypothesis. The whole question of how 'intentional' constructs are set up, and how modified, is, up to today, untouched by even the most primitive exploratory investigations.

Objectivity, in its adequate understanding, is thus fixed as a kind of ideal point, necessary for purposes of thought, but it is a virtual point towards which we are constantly striving, and which is quite unattainable. We are always sunk in relativity, and the danger is (relativity being our element) of slipping into a relativity which has forgotten that it is such. There are many forces acting upon the individual to reassure him about the existence of pure objectivity, but if these forces succeed in convincing the individual, they distort his entire conceptual orientation from that moment.

Nevertheless, we attain a peculiar form of cultural achievement in keeping our pictures of objectivity very roughly similar. Aberration is, beyond a certain point, visibly such. Yet, before that barrier between the acceptable and the simply eccentric is crossed, there is a vast hinterland of imprecision.

Applying these simple and evident verities to the realm of thought, ethics, politics, human relationships, it is evident that we are all working to a rule of thumb and hoping that nothing will go too badly wrong. We have no certainty that the way we go about projecting and operating the world is the best we could achieve, but while further investigations are going on, we proceed from day to day pretty much 'in character'. That is to say, we muddle through, posing as objectively qualified where called upon to appear so, and hiding the gaps and imprecisions in our picture of the world as best we can. The highest

aim of a great mass of people is, indeed, to conform absolutely to a rigidly fixed objectivity in which they are
socially stuck, and from which they dread to fall. Their
whole efforts are thus spent in managing to fit their picture of objectivity in with that dominantly held by the
group in which they are, such that no deviations or irregu-
larities are evident in their behaviour, opinions and life.

Is adequate objectivity even possible in questions concerning ethics and politics? The question as to what Protagoras really *meant* becomes, in the light or obscurity
of this question, ever more intriguing. When Protagoras
was quoted as saying that each of us (man) is the measure
of all things, he meant that the world appears to each of
us differently. It seemed to Plato that if Protagoras meant
by this famous opinion that all opinions and judgements
are equally valid, then he must be wrong.* But suppose he
did not mean that.

Suppose Protagoras meant that, even if my views on
matters of fact, opinion and logic are corrigible, that
nevertheless there is a fundamental relativity in which we
are sunk. Even our 'elders and betters' in matters of argument and judgement are still themselves only the measure
of all things. Even those who show themselves to know
more about something, to have more ability at something,
to be able to argue something more cogently, are themselves only hopelessly sunk in relativity in some more pro-
ficient way – a relativity which covers the best and the
worst with equal mercy and equal indifference. Husserl

---

* Plato's *Theaetetus* is in fact a disaster. Plato cannot refute
Protagoras's argument without the Forms – and the Forms, of
course, do not exist. But the fact that Plato *believes* in the Forms
is an argument in favour of Protagoras's contention that 'man is
the measure of all things, of things that are, that they are, and of
things that are not, that they are not'!

suggested in *Crisis* that we ought to re-examine Protagoras's views, bearing in mind the possibility that he had opened up an entire new dimension in thinking of which we have never taken advantage.

For it is evident that, just as the phenomena of the external world are experienced and 'intended' perspectivally, so the phenomena of ethical and political debate are experienced and 'intended' from a certain point of view, that point of view being the centre of an arc or fan of irradiating perspectives.

What are taken as 'facts', for example, by one party in an ethical or political debate may very well be questioned as 'facts' by the opposition. This is a direct function of perspective. Gabo's 'Spherical Theme', moved into the ethical–political field, yields us the following example.

Recently a film showing the living and working conditions of black South Africans in South Africa was shown on television. It was followed by a discussion between two of the men concerned with its production (both black) and three critics (all white) who had either visited South Africa or who had been involved in business with it.

The white critics were quick to dismiss the film, on the ground that it distorted 'the facts'. One of the 'facts' alleged to have been distorted was the claim, made by the producers of the film, that the shooting of the film had involved considerable personal risk, and that discovery would have meant imprisonment or worse.

The white critic asserted that this 'fact' about the physical danger of filming in South Africa was false (i.e. a non-fact) on the grounds that he himself, while on a recent visit to South Africa, had been freely allowed to use his camera there during the tour.

This raises the dual question of 'facts' and of perspectives in an acute form. To a black South African, the open use of a camera to film working conditions in the mines and in the servants' quarters of white homes in South Africa is physically dangerous: that to him is a 'fact'.

To a visiting white businessman, who would not anyway be photographing the same sort of thing, nor with the same intentions, the use of his Kodak round and about town was not objected to, and he was in no danger at all in filming what he saw: that for him is a 'fact'.

What do these two 'facts' have in common? The single common element is: *the use of a camera in South Africa*. That is the kernel of the 'fact', and if that is all we had to go on, we might very well be puzzled that two men could make such contradictory statements about it.

But the 'fact' is seen of course from two different perspectives, which make the 'fact' into a morally charged opposition, which itself operates only at the subjective level. For the black South African, *the use of a camera in South Africa* (kernel) means imprisonment, interrogation, perhaps death (perspective). For the white businessman, visiting as a VIP, *the use of a camera in South Africa* (kernel) is no more dangerous than the use of a camera in Hyde Park (perspective).

The 'fact' in question here can thus be broken down into its component parts as follows:
(1) kernel
(2) perspective from which it is seen
(3) interpretation of it
(4) use to be made of it

These subdivisions of what is proffered by each side as a unitary 'fact' occur because a fact can exist in two major modalities. A fact may be morally indifferent or it may be morally charged.

Simply because morally indifferent facts *are* morally indifferent, it has been too long assumed that morally charged facts are facts in the same unambiguous sense as the morally indifferent ones. A whole false objectivity springs from this simple act of bad faith. I can say: the Eiffel Tower is in Paris, and I can say: there is *apartheid* in South Africa. Both are facts. But the modality of these two facts means that, while we shall all discuss the Eiffel Tower amicably enough, the first sentence about the second fact is going to involve the perspectival question. We are immediately plunged into the world of subjectivity, and it is a false or a cheap objectivity which claims that it is going to discuss the second proposition ('fact') with complete objective detachment. If the 'fact' is morally charged, it therefore follows that no one who feels it to be morally charged is going to be able to discuss it with full objectivity.

The realm of morally indifferent facts is, of course, preeminently, that of mathematics, physics, etc. But we have to set them aside as a false paradigm.*

We can also ignore that vast mass of facts which are morally indifferent. Evidently there is a difficulty in drawing a line between morally charged and morally indifferent facts – everyone will want to draw the line here or there at different times and in different circumstances. But the fact that there is dawn and that there is twilight does not mean that we cannot in practice distinguish between night and day. There are, indeed, a whole mass of facts which do not ever directly concern us, as contributors to the communalized inter-subjective world, in a moral sense.

There remains that massive range of morally charged facts, the majority of which we have to deal with daily.

---

* Husserl's reasons for doing so are given in *Crisis*. His analysis has been elegantly supplemented, more recently, by Stephen Toulmin, in *The Uses of Argument*, Cambridge University Press, 1958.

And of these facts, the modality must, in the interests of adequate objectivity, be established, when these facts are deployed or debated in the political, ethical or philosophical arena.

There are still people who claim to be objective, even when arguing about things which affect them deeply. To take into account all the factors which make objective argument more or less impossible is a chastening business.

Firstly, what one takes to be true, evident, obvious, is a function of perspective – it depends upon the angle of vision upon the world and the quantity of phenomena which have been included in the purview.

Then there is the matter of subjective appropriation. How 'open' or 'closed' is one to new perspectives? Is one's own *parti pris* consciously present, or is one ignorant of the degree and kind of distortion in one's arrangement and presentation of the 'facts'?

There are no facts about the world (morally charged facts) which are not already instinct with a possible *use*. People get interested in a fact when they see a possibility of adding weight to an argument with which they themselves are deeply involved.

Then there is the question of gain and loss, of hope and fear. All these distort. We select and arrange our phenomena in accordance with our deepest fears or ambitions or both. Very often we are concerned not to find out what is true, but what will best support the argument or cause to which we are known to adhere, or which will show us up to be the brighter or the better man.

Everything selected for the purposes of the argument, everything useful for the argument, is filtered through the affective constitution of the individual. This affective construction is already in existence. Our experience of the outer world modifies that structure and affects the way it

works. By a process of selection and exclusion, a world-view which is helpful and advantageous will be filtered through the hopes and fears, the expectations and the experiences of the subjective existing individual. What finally gets through to the centre is a set of perspectives which have been multiply modified in the transmission.

There is also the question of one's own private perspectival history, which beds down and receives a lasting shape. Every day we filter through a certain set of perspectives (the advantageous or pleasant ones) and these integrate and stick together. We get used to them, they mould us to receiving a certain kind of perspectival reality tomorrow. What is true for the individual is true for him because his precedent perspectival history has shaped him into the man he is. When he argues, he takes up a position at the centre of his perspectival history, and manipulates his argument from there. Very often he even insists that he is being objective.

Above all, what is accepted as true is accepted as true because of an already existing structure of *belief* in the individual, an existing structure of interest or fear. It is to a person who already exists, complete in his hopes and fears, complete in his perspectival history, that one addresses one's arguments. He possesses already a vision of the world, a vision peculiarly his, which he has built up over the years with care and concern. What he does not want to understand, he will not accord the status of an argument. What runs against his interests, is not a 'fact'. What is antipathetic to his own view, is 'not objective'. What he disapproves of, is immoral. What he does, is right. What he stands for, is not to be questioned. The answer to Pilate's famous question is that there is no truth, only truths – and that the truth-perspectives of the Galilean carpenter and the truth-perspectives of the

Roman provincial governor cannot easily be reconciled, far less coincide.

Misled, misused, abused, by the logico-mathematical paradigm of facts and objectivity, we have too long tried to pretend that morally charged facts can be dealt with in the clinical manner appropriate to morally indifferent ones.

Once we have become aware of the peculiar nature of the problem, we become aware of the necessity of a new *type* of reflection, a mode of reflection which would do justice to the multiplicity of phenomena that have to be taken up into one synthetic conceptual solution. This type of thinking has not got a name. Its method is new and untried simply because the sheer difficulty of the problem has not been adequately faced before. Objectivity has always succeeded in dealing with selected parts of any problem, thus avoiding the painful necessity of taking the whole fragmented, perspectival, kaleidoscopic horizon of problems as inter-related parts of the one problem we need to solve. This is the meaning of Husserl's reference to Protagoras, no doubt.*

The perspectival world, the relativity of fact and event, of opinion and belief, imply a method of thinking which is peculiarly of our time, a thinking itself widely-stretched and catholic, both sympathetic and critical, associative and disjunctive, comparative and totalizing. This kind of thinking has not yet got a name. The necessity of its being brought into existence is urgent.

Subjective reflection, or subjective method (let us refer to this new form of thinking by these names for the moment), consists of first analysing, and then forcing a recognition of, perspectival reality and the relativity of criteria. Its job is then partly analytic and partly applied.

* *Crisis*, p. 165.

The Perspectival World and Subjective Method

Objectivity, with its preconception about the monolithic nature of truth, the facts, etc., is incapable of carrying out the kinds of jobs that subjective reflection can do. For the very belief that there is one and one only solution to any given problem or state of affairs implies that there is a distortion of adequate conceptuality from the outset. As the masses of contradictory data pile up, and objectivity still seems to be totally unaware of the lacunae in its own manner of approaching its problems, so the necessity of some other method of thinking, some more subjective and comparative method, becomes evident.

Subjective reflection operates through a series of descending strata of involvement with the materials to be considered, as follows:

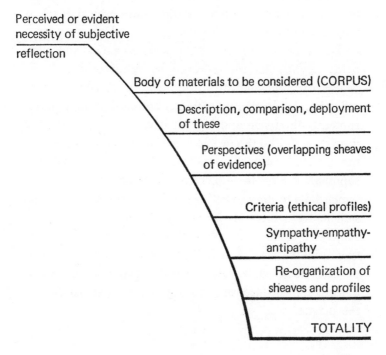

Perceived or evident
necessity of subjective
reflection

Body of materials to be considered (CORPUS)

Description, comparison, deployment
of these

Perspectives (overlapping sheaves
of evidence)

Criteria (ethical profiles)

Sympathy-empathy-
antipathy

Re-organization of
sheaves and profiles

TOTALITY

The word 'sheaves' is used to indicate the presence of 'bundles of relations', as Lévi-Strauss calls them. It is not isolated bits of information which count, but their continual re-occurence in significant groups. Likewise, 'profiles' are significantly differing shapes or contours of evidence. The scissor-artist cuts out profiles, no two of which are ever the same. Place one over the other, in a series, and significant differences will appear.

It is immediately evident that subjective reflection is working with subjective tools. Sympathy, empathy and antipathy, for instance, are not tools which would be allowed at any point in an objective analysis. Sympathy and empathy are perhaps unhappily chosen words, but their deployment in classical phenomenology* excuses their at least temporary retention. Antipathy as used here is as near as I can get to expressing a feeling of repulsion or refusal which operates at the same ethical level as empathy or sympathy : it guides the reflection away from certain solutions intuitively, just as empathy and sympathy might guide the reflection to certain others.

The diagram indicates the idea of a descent into reflection. Subjective reflection is not entirely or uninterruptedly discursive and logical. It can take time to sink deep enough into the problem, and integrate all aspects of the problem into the *totality*, which is the final and supreme reality in subjective thinking. Any thinking which fails to direct itself towards the totality fails to be sufficiently subjective. It will be evident from this that subjective thinking is not only just different from objective thinking, but is actually opposed to it, in that it devotes itself to a *total* solution, avoiding the usual objective, piece-meal or narrowly empirical approach like the plague.

* Max Scheler, Edith Stein, Theodor Lipps, Edmund Husserl.

The Perspectival World and Subjective Method

Subjective reflection cannot, of its very nature, be described in the fixities and definites of linguistic definitions. Many things enter into its course which are indefinable. It is for that reason that it serves an urgent present need, for the problems which objectivity cannot cope with are those which, being unquantifiable, contain many undefinable elements.

But some major structures of subjective thinking are evident from the start: personal commitment, ethical concern, desire to treat of the totality, necessity of taking account of the reality of perspectival variation and distortion, necessity of taking account of variations in operative criteria, the use of strange or unquantifiable collocations of evidence or information (such as sheaves and profiles), comparison, inter-relation, description, as well as sympathy, empathy and antipathy. These tools are no doubt a strange lot, but in my view they have a chance of dealing with complex problems in a way that objective tools do not.

Subjective method has a double task. The first is obviously analysis – a certain expertise in presenting the extreme heterogeneity of perspectival reality to its own reflection and understanding itself in terms of that – but it also has a second task. It has to force a recognition of the perspectival contradictions and incongruities upon an unwilling objective audience. There must be some kind of *discussion* of the implications of what subjective reflection arrives at, and it is primarily to objectivity, to the ruling *status quo* of opinion and sentiment, that subjective reflection must submit its results for urgent consideration.

Subjective method consists, then, first in analysis of a new and peculiar sort, and then in challenge to the old and the established objectivity. Subjective reflection aims at, hopes for, begs for, dialogue at some level which is not the usual scientific–objective evasiveness. There must be discussion, and subjective reflection should provide the materials which could be discussed. Objectivity is obviously quite incapable of providing any adequate materials for discussion, so subjectivity has to provoke the undesired dialogue.

The subjective reflection and method comes into being because of the inherent difficulty of dealing with many perspectival realities at once. In its effort to come at the whole, and to be faithful to the nature of the whole problem, it has to devise ways of holding in balance, holding in play, various sheaves or fans of conflicting evidence. It comes into being because these sheaves or fans of evidence are too complex to be dealt with by ordinary objective, empirical or quantifying methods. Since, then, it is perspectival reality (the fact that truth is multivalent and shifting) that brings subjective method into being, it is probably natural enough that its first concern, its first acts, its first reflective series, should concern perspectives themselves.

Evidently, perspectival reality is evanescent, shifting, difficult, personal, contradictory. The perspectival variation of reality (of what is asserted to be 'the truth', 'the case', 'the facts', 'the reality' about any given social or political phenomenon) is what has to be investigated first. The whole meaning and experienced reality of the intersubjective world is involved, the infinite interlocking of human intentionalities upon the world, and a system has to be found for organizing these into some kind of preliminary order.

Subjective method, then, starts with organizing sheaves of subjective evidence. It tries to clarify, first and foremost, how many angles of incidence there are on a problem in question, and the nature and content of these angles of incidence. Subjective analysis gathers subjective statements about the world (coming from various objective sources) and tries to make a careful comparison of them.

Subjective reflection assumes, as a working hypothesis, that, as in the 'Spherical Theme' of Gabo, a problem has a different construction when seen from various points in conceptual space. Presenting and comparing the various perspectives involved in a specific problem allows of a more flexible analysis of a problem which if persistently and rigidly (inflexibly) seen from one objective point of view would have appeared monolithic. In fact, the problem will always turn out to be the concatenation of a large number of inter-related issues.

To take an achieved analysis as an example: R. D. Laing's and A. Esterson's *Families of Schizophrenics.** Rather than treating a case of schizophrenia as *one* thing possessed by *one* person and regarded as *his or her* unique problem, Laing and Esterson tape-recorded interviews with the families of (the) schizophrenics (the title is obviously a rather savage grammatical joke), such that the versions, points of view, perspectives, of the family can be compared with each other and with the point of view or perspective of the patient himself. The results are startling, electrifying. Suddenly, by an astute collocation and comparison of the perspectives of the family and of the patient (which are always in flagrant contradiction) the actual reasons why this 'patient' became mentally unstable are revealed. Awful visual and verbal self-contradictions are set up in the parental perspectives, which clash not only with each other but with the perspective of the patient. It becomes glaringly obvious that 'reality',

* Vol. 1 of *Sanity, Madness and the Family*, Tavistock Press, 1964.

'objectivity' and so on have been pretty odd in this family of schizophrenics for many years, and that the weakest member of the team has (psychically) gone to the wall. So great, so persistent has been the distortion of 'reality' in this family (the reasons for this are usually a combination of religious bigotry, social conformism or reduced intelligence in general) that one member of the family has been unable to piece together the world into any coherent system at all. So, he or she has yielded to the easier state of mental disorientation, which Laing has elsewhere classified as a way of living through an unlivable situation.

Through the subjective method (Laing and Esterson in fact use roughly the tools I call description, comparison, deployment, perspectives, sympathy and re-organization of sheaves and profiles) the authors of this revolutionary study have managed to establish some truth about the *totality* of the psychic background of these families of schizophrenics. The totality is the major concern, and the totality is what is arrived at in analysis. But it is not arrived at by crude behaviourist quantification. It is arrived at by a canny, conscious, intelligent and organized deployment and comparison of perspectives. Each and every member of the family has his or her own 'version' of 'the truth', and each and every member is at variance, (sometimes, strikingly, on matters of 'fact') with each other about how things 'really' happened. For the reader of the book the sleuthing is pretty easy, as all the work has been done in advance by the sapient arrangers of subjective material. This is subjective method at its best, in that it succeeds in establishing the totality of truths about a lived situation by means of showing up the internal contradictions of any one objective account of that lived situation.

It will be clear that Laing and Esterson are using a

phenomenological approach, but there is nothing in it which is not also independent of phenomenology and couldn't be found somewhere in the categories of subjective reflection. The perspectival world was not, after all, first noticed by Husserl, nor even by Protagoras. Phenomenology and subjective reflection run parallel, but need not be the same thing. *The Divided Self*, for instance, is a pioneer work of applied subjective method, and works in proud independence of any heavy orthodox body of phenomenological theory, though one feels that most of this has been absorbed somewhere along the line, and been transformed from a knowledge into a stance or an attitude. Perhaps this is the best use phenomenology can be put to, since in its pure form it is more or less empirically useless.

Subjective method is a form of subjective thinking which is independent of the *fiats* of Husserl or any other phenomenologist. It is a form of thinking brought into existence by the exigencies of our modern world, and though phenomenology is the nearest theoretical relation it has, it is in fact a form of thinking *sui generis*. The elements of this sort of thinking are first to be noticed, for instance, not in the philosophical Schools, but in the world of the dissenting young. They have not found their concepts, but they are moving surely towards formulating them through the consistent use of their indirect communications.

Subjective reflection is in fact an advance upon phenomenology, as the example of Laing and Esterson makes clear. Subjective method can be applied and give results, whereas the embargoes of classical phenomenological theory are heavy indeed to bear.

If, for instance, we turn back to Husserl's own late attempts, in the fifth *Cartesian Meditation*, to deal with the inter-related problems of the Other, of inter-subjectivity, of the body, of the constitution of the Other in space by analogy and pairing, of perspectival reality and imaginative variation and so on, we find ourselves more hampered than helped by the excessively narrow and tight-fitting theoretical restrictions that Husserl (as usual) puts upon his reflections.

The fifth *Cartesian Meditation* is of course a major text in Husserl's work, forming with *Crisis* the high point of his thinking. But the restrictions of theoretical interest are maddeningly hard to bear if our concern is to work out any theory of perspectives that would help us analyse the world we live in. In his remark about 'free variations', for instance, we envisage a sudden hope that a means for transferring in conceptual space (such that I might see my 'here' (*hic*) from the position of the other's 'there' (*illic*) and vice versa) is being opened up for us. But Husserl takes away with his left hand what he offers with his right. We can indeed, by 'free variation' of *hic* and *illic* in conceptual space, come to realize that the angle of incidence upon the world is informatively different each time we carry out the 'free variations', but he points out that, even then, I shall only see from the other man's point of view what *I* would have seen from the same place. I shall never see what *he* saw, for he is an enigma, an unknowable constituting subjectivity whose perspectives on the world I have no means of knowing, however long I try: indeed, I can only grasp the veriest rudiments of what he must be seeing and intending by a brutally crude series of acts of 'pairing' and 'analogy'.

Ricoeur sums up admirably:

If it is true that the pairing of my *hic* with the *illic* of the Other is rendered less incomprehensible through the mediation of my potential experience ('if I were over there'), this pairing remains essentially an enigma, for the *hic* of the Other, just as it is for him, differs essentially from the *hic* which would be mine if I went over there. This 'over there' – insofar as it is a 'here' for the Other – does not belong, even potentially, to my own sphere. The 'as if I, myself, I were over there' does not permit introducing the here of the Other into my sphere. My here and the over there of the Other are mutually exclusive.*

In fact, checkmate. There is no way of knowing what the Other actually sees, feels, intends, *as if I were he*. Solipsism is an incurable state into which we are born. Husserl's phenomenology of the *Cartesian Meditations* in fact cuts us off into individual thinking monads just as radically as Descartes' *Meditations* do. Ricoeur adds consolingly, 'Husserl is his most admirable self when he brings out anew a difficulty which he seemed to have resolved.'†
Well, perhaps. But it does seem a terrible anti-climax to the massive build-up of Husserlian phenomenology.

But it is in the new clarity that we gain from Husserl's phenomenology that we can see the vital necessity of a subjective method. This method would not be phenomenological – how could it be, in view of Husserl's own admitted defeat in the area of inter-subjectivity? – but it could avail itself of much that Husserl established in order to push ahead into newer and more viable formulations of adequate subjective method.

The perspectival world was brought into prominence as a major philosophical task, as *the* major philosophical task, of our age, by Husserl. He himself failed to solve it,

* Paul Ricoeur, *Husserl, An Analysis of His Phenomenology*, Northwestern University Press, Evanston, 1967, p. 130.
† loc. cit.

indeed his first sketches show how easily the heavy machinery of his phenomenology can be brought to a dead halt. Nevertheless, Husserl's indication about what is the vital *problem* of our time is still valid: it is the evolution of a subjective method which would take account of the perspectival world and of inter-subjectivity in the cultural and moral communities in which we live. This remains the major problem. And it is the task of present-day reflection to come to an adequate, a comprehensive, level of inquiry, such that genuine subjective reflection and method can be evolved.

The greatest difficulty for subjective method is to *get going* after, and in spite of, Husserl. The insights of phenomenology have been generally admitted to be potentially immensely important – and this feeling is becoming ever stronger and more widespread. Yet those who engage in phenomenological reading tend never to re-emerge as practitioners. R. D. Laing is an exception, and an intensely significant one. For he has proved that one can grasp the essential truths of phenomenology, and *still* develop a specific subjective method suited to his particular terrain. Each and every human concern has to develop a subjective method in its own terms and for its own purposes, and it is obvious that what suits one discipline or art will not suit another in exactly those terms or in exactly the same way.

Laing's breakthrough in psychiatry has been accompanied, for instance, by John Hopkins's breakthrough in the medium of the TV play. There is no doubt that the subjective analysis, the concatenation and comparison of sheaves of perspectives and moral profiles, which John Hopkins has integrated in *Talking to a Stranger* is a significant happening in the development of a modern subjective reflection. Four people, four stories, four sets of eyes, four temporal and emotive histories, four 'accounts' of the same events, four interpretations of the same events, interwoven in four plays. What the viewer or reader of these four plays finally comes to is not 'the truth', 'the facts', but four ways of seeing 'the truth' and four experiences of the 'facts'. Common to both Hopkins's work and Laing's is this care for the level of perspectival evidence, the arrangement of significances, the slow patient effort at multiple unravelling.

Whichever way one comes at the task, then, the organization of perspectives will form the major part of any subjective thinking. The major difficulty is in deciding which interpretations of the world are significant in this case, and significant in respect to which others.

In this connection, the sheaves of evidence emanating from indirect communicators will be analysable for the first time. The indirect communicator, who exists his meaning in the world as a walking sign, cannot be understood except subjectively.

Great indirect communicators are aware of this, and issue their message in full consciousness of the level of response they are attempting to evoke.* But even unconscious indirect communicators, like the dissenting young, are aiming their messages at the deepest-lying strata of subjectivity in their fellow men. Even if their concepts are unclear or in process of change, their communication has a certain imperfect subjective force.

No objective interpretation of indirect communication is possible. Only subjective reflection can process it, and

---

* The most amazing example I know of is St John's Gospel, Chapter 18, verses 37 and 38. What are the *sorts* of subjective information offered by the relation of the latter part of verse 38 to the second part of verse 37; and of the whole of verse 38 to the whole of verse 37?

that reflection has itself to develop its own methods of processing.

As it descends through the perspectival morass of imprecisions and ambiguities, the subjective reflection encounters that deeper level of ethical profiles, of criteria, which have produced the perspectival realities. 'It is almost incredible that he should have done x believing it to be the right course of action, but, nevertheless, *on his criteria*, it must have seemed right to him.' This is a general form of a judgement that we make daily about something or other, but it usually never gets further than this, being a gesture of general head-wagging despondency about the confusion of other men's motives. (One's own, of course, are never called into question. Hence the situation, inter-subjectively, arises).

We are not always fully aware of the dangerous degree to which perspectival commitments and ethical criteria overlap, support and re-inforce each other. The only way of establishing the connexions in any given case is by examining the two sheaves of evidence separately.

A perspectival view of the world will be bolstered up by the criteria of action which best justify the sort of world accepted as right in that perspectival view. Subjective reflection begins by separating perspectives from criteria. The difficulty comes when it is a case of unravelling what belongs to the level of perspectives and what belongs to the level of ethical profiles. Most of the illogical, blatantly untrue or breathtakingly unacceptable things that are said result from a rapid and un-analysed transition from general world-view to ethical profile. The speaker is generally unaware of the immense damage he does to his own credibility in these moments, and if he is cynical enough or powerful enough, he does not care.

In politics, these transitions are familiar to us from the

daily papers and the TV screen. A reigning political objectivity will usually, for instance, refuse to produce its criteria of action (the value-judgements upon which its actions are based) on the grounds that doing so would damage its security, etc. This refusal actually indicates that a given objectivity refuses to be explicit about its ethical profile – and does so in a particularly cagey way, for its general perspectival view of the world is clear enough. There is thus a clear gap set up between the perspectival reality of that objectivity and the ethical profile which underlies it, but to which it will not admit.

What is at stake in such a refusal to discuss criteria is the suspicion that such a discussion would expose the reality behind the political *status quo*, that a criterion not named has not yet been acknowledged. Therefore, a cagey objectivity which does not want to lay its ethical cards down on the table equivocates at the level of its world-view (security, discussions in progress, 'facts' not yet established, etc., etc.).

Subjective method has to work out devices by which the glaring discrepancy between official spiel and authentic motive can be brought up to the level of clear evidence and imposed as a discussion upon those who, in their assured objectivity, are most unwilling to hear it. This needs careful, conscious and painstaking work.

One of the major tasks of subjective method is to establish rules for the collecting, arranging and comparison of ethical profiles. Profiles never fit over one another exactly. The differences between one profile and the succeeding one is vital: it indicates a direction which the subjective research must follow.

It is an ungrateful task to defend sympathy, empathy and antipathy at a high-flown methodological level. These are not realities which can very well be discussed in a cool table of contents, but they form an essential part of subjective method. Just as the rationalist tradition insists on the exclusion of the thinker from the thought, so must the subjective thinker, who is deeply subjective, in the sense of moral concern, insist on his inclusion.

The place of these intuitive phenomena in a subjective analysis is not merely gratuitous, however. Without them the analysis would not proceed, would not know its own path, would not have a sufficient *raison d'être* for continuing. Intuitive participation in the act of thought gives a value, a personal value, to the whole enterprise. It guides the thinker towards a new clarity and warns him off conclusions which are less than adequate in the light of the totality.

Further one need not go. Sympathy and antipathy are not elements one can include or exclude at will: they are inevitable structural parts of a whole thinking being.

Finally, subjective method can only work in terms of the *totality* of available or relevant phenomena. The totality is actually the life-world we live in, and our duties are to it. It is the concept of the totality, to which we are responsible, that makes of the subjective method a powerful integrational device.

It refuses the parts, taken in isolation. It insists upon the full setting-up of any problem, including the subjective factors, duly acknowledged as such. It refuses to reduce the whole to any grid, schema or model (Gestalt: 'There are wholes, the behaviour of which is not determined by that of their individual elements, but where the part-processes are themselves determined by the intrinsic nature of the whole,' etc.). It opposes reductive methodology in all its forms. It could be a powerful force for good in all the human sciences, especially in psychology where the living totality would be accepted as the minimal phenomenon of study, but equally beneficial in others, including sociology, politics, literature and philosophy.

It seems an almost impossible demand. Certainly objectivity will be quick to point out the difficulties of taking the whole problem as the minimal unit.

But if the totality is interpreted as being the world, the life-world, then the importance of thinking in terms of it is becoming daily more striking. Subjective method, in its concern for the totality, points to the two most glaring insouciances in current objectivity. Political objectivity has to come to terms with its own crazy irrationality, and scientific objectivity has to come to terms with its ever-increasing proliferation of context-less achievements.

What are context-less achievements? They are local scientific successes which precede even the remotest notion of how to deal with them ethically or how to integrate them into the needs of the totality. Context-less achievements are scientific successes whose bearing on human beings in the world has never, during the long years of research, been examined or even questioned. They represent, in the light of the totality, temporary failures of adequate objectivity.

There is at the moment no science, no field of human activity, where the dispossession of the totality in favour of the parts is not taking place. The fight against behaviourist reductionism is, as Konrad Lorenz says, rather quixotic, and naturally enough few undertake that fight.

But modern subjectivity in all its forms is in fact appealing, though in loosely articulated ways, to the idea of the totality. Science and philosophy are tending ever more in one direction, subjectivity in the world in the directly contrary direction. Ever greater formalization, ever greater reduction of totality to parts is in fact opposed by a growing spiritual need for a total science, which would include man in it. Subjectivity aims at a philosophy of the whole man, of a whole experience, of the whole world. Subjectivity is in fact a totality philosophy, even if only implicitly. Therein lies its strength – and its weakness.

Various philosophies of the totality already exist, of course, and their attractiveness is evident, even if the philosophers of the West find this curious. The sympathy of the young romantics is obviously for the totality philosophy of Communism, if not in its Marxist–Leninist forms, then at least in its Castro–Guevara–Mao form. There is a strong element of spiritual transcendence included in the later forms of Communism, a trenchant humour too, an almost swashbuckling devil-may-care fittedness to the world which makes it attractive to those disillusioned by the severer forms of Communism and by their own political system.

That dreaming spirit, that openness to the totality, results directly from the failure of our own objective philosophy to formulate a sufficiently total philosophy of the individual in our time. The official doctrine of behaviourist and positivist reduction plays straight into the hands of the opposing ideology whose completeness of explanation and ethical commitment to the cause of the totality is visibly seen to be effective in great areas of the globe.

Indeed, if one were to compare the ethical attitudes of the young romantics and of our own political systems, it becomes clear that the first are dreaming of the totality and acting piecemeal, while the latter are thinking piecemeal and acting in a totalitarian manner.

Such an opposition at the centre of our rationality obviously contains within itself the seeds of destruction. It is quite impolitic, not to say quite irrational, to have the politicians and the scientists holding to one model of rationality while vast quantities of the population hold to another. This phenomenon is not only visible in the West, it lies beneath the revolutions in Czechoslovakia and Poland, the literature of Pasternak, Yevtushenko, Solzhenitsyn and Amalrik, not to mention large sections of the scientific community in Russia itself, as a potent agent for the destruction of the unity of the official Communist orthodoxy. The fact that Communism will certainly fall divided does not make it any more pleasant to contemplate the very high probability that America will do the same.

Subjective method is the patient unravelling of the contradictions inherent in the idea of *two* objectivities in one society: one objectivity excluding the human being from the totality and the other insisting that he should be included in it. If subjective critique does not very soon begin to show its successes, the dreaming spirit in love with totality will itself bring down our science and our society in fragments.

Subjective method is thus the only way of preventing an outright clash between subjectivity constituted as irrationalism or terrorism, and objectivity constituted as the political–scientific orthodoxy of the Right.

If there is even a possibility that this subjectively integrated rationality could be achieved, if the panic fear with which current objectivity reacts to subjective critique at the moment could be replaced by a more harmonious relationship between the various parts of human reason, then the usefulness of the subjective method cannot be questioned at this time by anyone who is humanly concerned for the cause of rationality.

6

PHILOSOPHICAL
SPACE

Every age has its characteristic conceptual space. Montaigne wrote his essays in a small room, twelve paces across, in a tower from the windows of which he could stare down into a perfectly formal French Renaissance garden. The rolling acres of vines belonging to the *château* of Montaigne sweep away to the horizons on every side, on the west towards Bordeaux where Montaigne was Mayor.

It was not an entirely free space, for the age of Montaigne suffered many reserves and blockages, but it was a possessed, orderly space, with clear limits and known qualities. It was a space which Montaigne shared with Pascal, the space which, somewhere in the majesty of the heaven, contained God and his angels in Paradise.

The mathematical rationalism of Descartes wrested that happy view of space from both of them. The narrow confines of the age of reason began to pinch and then to hurt. 'The eternal silence of those infinite spaces casts me into dread,' confided Pascal to his diary. Space for Pascal, now incapable of holding God, becomes the inner cramping space of fear.

Kant's space is the narrow one of his age, the tiny limits of Koenigsberg, which he never left in his life, and the cramping restrictiveness of a human reason which prided itself on knowing everything. Only when Kant feels within him the wonder for the starry heavens above and the moral law within does he escape the narrow constrictions of his age.

The space of the Romantic age opens out again. Vast shadowy imaginative landscapes of the mind, reverie, feeling, absorption, mystery, the limitless, the unknown. Within this wide landscape of the mind, moral phenomena stand out with tremendous insistence. Fichte's space is the space of encounter. Two humans beings, incarnated in their bodies, meet each other on the human terrain of rights and duties. Philosophy's whole aim shall be to understand these things adequately. Respect for the other as incarnated subjectivity opens up a new dimension of human thinking.

This dimension was given physical exemplification in the life of Søren Kierkegaard. In the narrow streets and squares of Copenhagen, the indirect communication was brought into being. Incarnated subjectivity becomes a walking sign, and the space of thinking opens out yet again on every side.

In our own age Heidegger, quoting Novalis, defines philosophy as a homesickness, a longing for a land far from here. Restless and dissatisfied, we attempt to return to the sources of our own understanding, in vain. The whole of Being has become our province, and it is too small. Being transcends us. Only in perusing the poets may we hope to find some consolation for our loss. Space has become inner, the world is inner and so is the source. We are thus the locus of space, and as such have become the shepherds of Being.

Every thinker brings a space into being which he establishes as peculiarly his own. It has its own limits, its own sudden openings-out onto the void, its own content, its own terms of reference, its own aims and its own necessity. Fichte observed that the type of philosophy a man chooses will depend on the type of man he is. In this free-ing observation, Fichte opens out a new dimension for us to explore: dare we really believe that we may *choose* which philosophy we need?

The characteristic thought-condition of our age is space-lessness: pressure.

So much in the modern world forces us to the conclu-sion that philosophy is something done by the profes-sionals in the universities, like strategy is something done by strategists in the Pentagon or the Kremlin, such that we have inwardly died to the possibility of thinking for ourselves, of demanding a philosophy that *we* want. We have been browbeaten and bullied into expecting our philosophy to be handed out from above, like our military policies, our politics, our daily bread and the complete list of permissible thoughts.

But if the type of philosophy that a man chooses de-pends on the type of man he is, then each and every one of us has a right to a philosophy of his own, a right to a space he can think in, a right to his own subjective thought-world.

It is a daring contention. The massed expertise of the professionals will of course oppose it to the last ditch. To assert that subjectively chosen conceptual space is open to each and every thinking being is, in our age, tanta-mount to treason against the State. Dare we, neverthe-less, think it, assert it, to be true?

Just how one wins through to a space one can think in involves a very interesting series of conceptual transfor-mations. Necessarily, one starts from somewhere. Some thinker, some writer, some person in the world who com-municates indirectly, is our starting point. If we begin to think that theory through, we come to a point where the original spatiality of the thought-system has to be transformed into a new personal one.

Suppose one begins by reading a certain philosopher or novelist. His space, the limits of his world, are for the time being, accepted on trust while we explore that world. Every term he uses, every assumption he makes, refers to the architecture of his system, refers to the structure that he is bringing into being through his writing. For the first part of our reading and thinking we are completely passive, absorbing.

Then we begin to transform his terms into our terms A cross-fertilization of two lived spaces begins to happen, a strange spatial mutation takes place, a symbiosis. I begin to inter-penetrate into that space, my space, my thought-world begins to happen alongside the other man's and I am suddenly 'understanding' him. His space is acceptable to me, it is freeing and not cramping (otherwise this symbiosis would never have got started) and I am beginning to 'get the feel' of this system of thought. I can predict certain dimensions of it, I can feel myself into its space, I can rely on it. Above all, it helps me to think. I grow in capability as I read. I can take certain hurdles I couldn't take before. Fear decreases.

Then finally the terms in which he is expressing himself have to be transformed into my terms. When Descartes writes, for instance, 'It is at least as certain that God, who is this perfect being, is, or exists, as any demonstration of geometry can be' (*Discourse on Method*, Part 4), I have to reorganize the space of Descartes' system such that I can understand this proposition at all, such that I can see something which makes sense (to me) in what appears to be nonsense. Most of the propositions of the fourth part of the *Discourse* have to be re-potentiated in this way. I have to rearrange the terms in which Descartes expresses himself, in order that I can grasp what he is trying to show me about the *Cogito*. If I want to under-stand *that*, I have no choice but to re-order the Cartesian disposition of terms and concepts such as they occur on the page.

This re-ordering of terms is in fact a re-ordering of spatiality. Descartes' system includes a harmonious inter-change between mathematical and theological certainties, mine does not. Descartes is making a logical point at this juncture of his *Discourse* (the idea of a triangle does not include existence, but the idea of a Perfect Being does), so I have to adapt a space which includes the idea of Perfect Beings to a space which does not. Do I have to admit that I do not 'understand' Descartes if I do not happen to believe in the idea of a Perfect Being? Or do I not simply trans-form what I take him to be saying, in theological space, into terms which have some meaning in a space which remains resolutely earthbound? Obviously the latter.

A final judgement on a specific philosophical problem cannot be made at any level higher than that of the in-tuitive judging consciousness of the individual. Either understanding becomes existential, or it does not come at all. There is no specifically 'philosophical' faculty of the mind in which or through which a dilemma can be finally, once and for all, solved, *aufgehoben*, done away with. Even at the limits of our inquiries we are only judging ac-cording to our lights, as best we can.

There is no final act of judgement, either, just as there is no greatest prime number. One more can be added, will be added, has already been added. However careful the analysis has been, up to and including the moment when we make our 'decision', that last thought-act is a personal judgement of the whole precedent series. It is an act of affirmation or dissent. I say to myself: 'This I believe to be the case', or 'I do not believe that this is the case', and with such an affirmation or dissent, the philosophical space thus enclosed belongs to me existentially.

Since it so clearly involves commitment or choice at the end, the entire process is seen, retrospectively, to have been ethical. Every little decision on the way was a modification, was a new moment in the process of becoming. The thinker shapes himself as he thinks. He excludes or includes, he modifies the shape of his world. Philosophical space is thus the space of choice. The thinker has to decide not only what is right and wrong but also what he wants to *become* by deciding the matter this way rather than that way. In deciding what he wants to become, he decides indirectly what he wants his world to become. All thinking is legislative.

The vital moment in this process of transformation is when the *alternatives* offered in a preceding system have to be *rejected*.

Thinking is doubly ethical. First it involves transforming the terms of a thinker's system into terms which can be grasped, comprehended and re-deployed in one's own system. And then, in a second moment, thinking has to refuse certain terms in the original system, certain alternatives, certain propositions, certain assumptions. Thinking has to become independent enough not only to understand the law, but to change it.

It is sobering to realize to what an extent we inherit our problems from our predecessors rather than finding out from experience what our contemporary problems really are. We are conditioned historically through and through, as Husserl observes, and we tend to think therefore that the important problems, the ones that need solving, are the ones that are handed down to us as significant.

In these inherited problems, there are things which absolutely refuse to be solved in the terms in which they are formulated. Things stick, jam, lock and will not come apart. There are traditional conundrums, traditional procedures, traditional ways of tackling traditional problems, such that, from generation to generation, the idle debate goes on.

Not a single debate at present going on in our philosophical Schools, for instance, has arisen from the crisis of the world we live in, but all have been inherited from the pundits of the 1920s and 1930s.

The situation perpetuates itself largely (but not exclusively) because the terms in which a problem is cast are inherited along with the conundrum. We were not asked, for a long period in our history, whether we are free, or, in what senses are we free but we were asked whether we have *free will*. Until those two terms are torn apart, I defy anyone to answer the question, or even to make sense of it. There are dozens of these traditional binary chestnuts. What is malign about them is their inescapably binary formulation.

And in our modern world we are ceaselessly being asked to choose between two things, parties, policies, procedures, *neither of which is acceptable.*

This is where philosophical space (as opposed to the current philosophical *pressure*) becomes a life-necessity. In genuine, personally won philosophical space, all choice-pairs, all alternatives, of which both terms are irreceivable, would be excluded. The question would have to be reformulated before any answer was sought.* It means

* Does one have to give examples? There are so many daily. For instance: do you want to send arms to South Africa, or do you want the Indian Ocean to be a Russian lake? Do you want to fight in Vietnam, or do you want the whole of the world Communist? Do you want to live in a white world, or do you want to be overrun by the blacks? etc., etc.

growing up, and daring to be fully responsible for one's thoughts and acts.

In other words, in a genuinely free philosophical space, a space where one was free to think and be oneself in thinking, one chooses which problems one will deal with, *and in which terms*. So many ways of asking the question foreclose the issue and leave the individual nothing but a rubber-stamping job to do. This would be resisted in an adequate, an open, space. One would not accept being bullied and chivvied into facing a problem in a way which utterly hamstrings the individual who is asked. One would demand that the question be put some other way, *a way which offered a possible solution, a solution valid in terms of the totality.*

An interesting example of an achieved refusal of invalid terms in a choice-pair comes from that brave and independent thinker, Georg Lukács. Although he was concerned, in *The Meaning of Contemporary Realism,** with literature, he thinks in terms of the political and ethical totality which literature implies. Lukács has dared to construct and to inhabit his own philosophical space, and since his achievement is a proof that the thing can be done, it is perhaps worth just glancing at the terms of his double refusal.

Concerned to reject 'modernism' in literature, a 'modernism' which expresses, in its obsessive cultivation of technique and *Angst*, a total refusal to integrate itself into any adequate understanding of history, Lukács yet refuses as well the apparent 'alternative', socialist realism. This he finds as short in art as 'modernist' art is short in socialism.

If Lukács, then, demands 'more matter with less art' of Joyce, Woolf, Beckett and Kafka, he still finds much

* Merlin Press, London, 1963.

socialist realism inadequate for anything but propaganda purposes. He can accept neither the one nor the other, as they stand.

It is a refusal to be fobbed off with an inadequate pair of terms to choose from. Lukács casts round for some *alternative to the alternative*. He lights on Solzhenitsyn. There, he says, is a living exemplar of a sufficient realism who is also a great artist. Like Thomas Mann's, his canvas includes the totality of the social conditions of his day, from top to bottom, from left to right, and the whole is art of the highest order. In that achievement, historically adequate realism which is yet artistically qualified to reflect Soviet orthodoxy and the official party line, Lukács sees the opening up of the correct terms of argument, and the solution of a problem which, as argued officially, is as sterile as it is banal.

Lukács's book might be taken as an exemplary case of owned philosophical space. In that space, he is free to reject existing and inadequate thought-pairs. Since thought is an ethical business, bearing on the totality, and since the terms of the argument, as offered, are both inadequate and unacceptable, then they both have to be rejected straight away and a better formulation sought. This is only possible in personally owned and controlled philosophical space. If one has that, one can still be a free man, even in Hungary.

Ethics and politics desperately need to be liberated from the terms in which they are traditionally discussed. We have to invent new formulations for our problems, ruthlessly rejecting formulations of 'what is wrong', which do not in fact bear even remotely upon what *is* wrong, because the terms we are offered in which to discuss these problems are counters of self-interest or quantifying positivism in the first place. In a controlled philosophical space, in that concern for the totality which we have progressively tried to define as deep subjectivity, formulations would be evolved for the real problems, and an attempt made to solve those problems, in a way which insists on being resolutely independent of the terms in which the problems are traditionally presented.

One major advance in reformulating problems would be to scrutinize their emergence in *series*, and *series of series*. The true structure of our problems would be discerned in terms of the series in which they appear. Hence, if four different sets of events, four connected sets of profiles, happen, in the course of a certain period of time, in some such pattern as this:

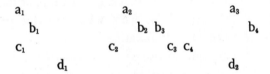

then it is in terms of these series, and the inter-relationships between one series and another, that the problem in fact exists. The series can be read horizontally, diagonally, or in depth, according to informational potential.

Philosophical space is the space of interpretative freedom. Freedom is reserved, that is to say, by the analyst, to make what connections *he* thinks are the relevant ones. His freedom is a *combinative* freedom. Some of the relationships in the series will have to be discerned in spite of the flow of current received opinion, or in spite of the hostility of objectivity, which will deny flatly that certain series have anything to do with certain other series. Nevertheless, there is no series of profiles which is not connected to all the others, at some interpretative level. Series are groups of what there is to be observed in the world and there can be no series which is external to the

totality. What there is in space is what there is, psychically.

Since freedom is attributed to the agent, in philosophical space, and with it full responsibility for what he does,
so the analyst, in his responsibility, uses the privilege of
unfettered combinative possibilities for such juxtaposition
of series as *he* thinks will give the most illuminating and
far-reaching results. He has to fight for this privilege all
the time, for the privilege of thinking and combining evidence for himself.

The subjective analyst is not, of course, analysing series
for nothing: he is analysing because these particular series
of events or profiles concern him personally. There is
therefore an interpenetration, a criss-crossing, of the free-
ranging subjectivity of the agent who emits the profiles,
and the free-ranging combinative faculty of the analyst.
There is a new kind of empathetic, totalizing, grasp of
reality, which is allowed to lead where it has to. To
achieve this, it has to break free of the servitude of the
terms in which problems are traditionally or officially presented to it.

Philosophical space is not only, then, a personally won
space to think in, not only a transformation of existing
thinkers' systems into one's own, not only the refusal of
false alternatives and the search for a viable statement of
problems, but also a space of research and reflection.

What marks it off and distinguishes it from the pres-
surized spacelessness we normally have to 'think' in is its
attribution of freedom both to the agent and to the
analyst. It is only in philosophical space, that is to say,
that the perspectives and profiles of the living human subject get adequate analysis. Behaviourist reductionism
(which is the intellectual climate of our time) de-spatializes
the phenomena from the outset and as a result of that,

ethical space ceases to exist as an arena of intentional *meaning*. When we call space philosophical, therefore, we do so in the fully conscious intention of distinguishing that sort of interpretative space, the space of reflective freedom and combinative liberty, from behaviourist-positivist spacelessness, the pan-determinism of reductive quantification.

For it is only in philosophical space that ethical space can be retained, preserved and understood. And it is only in philosophical space that the other is accorded that total respect which is due to him as an embodied subjectivity. And since that is the fundamental principle of all ethics, the preservation of that fundamental principle depends upon the preservation of philosophical space.

It takes a jump of a quite unusual kind to train oneself to think subjectively, so great is the prestige of objective thinking. The very possibility, indeed, of subjective thinking will doubtless be challenged.

But that challenge cannot affect its reality, for subjectivity has merged with thought in this century. It can be done, and it ought to be done. For only by defining the problems subjectively will philosophical space, the space in which genuine human problems are adequately conceived, come into existence.

In a genuine philosophical space, it would be possible to discuss which criteria are binding upon us all in the life-world, and in which way action can best serve the interests of the totality.

In philosophical space, the great mass of individuals now numbed into silence and inanition would not only have viable alternatives of action offered to them, but also be offered adequate criteria to justify such action. They would have a voice in the conduct of affairs and participate in the way things are directed.

Towards Deep Subjectivity

Deep subjectivity emerges finally then as a concern for objectivity, for a full, real and adequate objectivity. In order to express this concern, it has to discover (first of all) and then to trust to (even harder) a space of personally won philosophical commitment.

Deep subjectivity operates from within this philosophical space with the tools of subjective analysis and critique. It thus affects and challenges the world of objectivity and sets up a more acceptable standard of objectivity beside it.

Everything remains to be done, and time is growing short.

72 73 74 75 12 11 10 9 8 7 6 5 4 3 2 1